The World's Cheapest Destinations

21 Countries Where Your Money is Worth a Fortune

Fourth Edition

Published by BookLocker.com, Inc., Bradenton, Florida.

Printed in the United States of America on acid-free paper.

Booklocker.com, Inc.
2013

Fourth Edition

The World's Cheapest Destinations

21 Countries Where Your Money is Worth a Fortune

Fourth Edition

Tim Leffel

What others have to say:

"Tim Leffel has long been a guru of balancing the practicalities of cheap travel with a keen sense of judgment about the aesthetic value offered by varied countries around the world. In this newly researched and expanded edition, Tim's easy conversational style turns the book into a page-turner, leaving you hungry to set off on the many paths he opens up to the traveler's imagination."
- Gregory Hubbs, editor-in-chief, TransitionsAbroad.com.

"The very first step to saving money when on the road is to figure out where you can stretch your money the furthest. Due to the ebb and flow of international finance, wars, and natural disasters... the cheapest places are always changing. Tim offers a great way to hit this moving target."
- Doug Lansky, author of more than 10 travel books including *First Time Around the World*

"Leffel wastes no time outlining some of the world's cheapest destinations in a concise and honest fashion. Refreshingly pointed, this compact guide is an ideal handbook for those looking to stretch their money further."
- Stuart McDonald, editor of Travelfish.org

"This is a great book for new travelers or for want-to-be backpackers. Tim gives a great rundown of destinations that are easier, safer and tastier than you may think. The local tourism board may not always agree with his honest assessments, but you should appreciate them. Update your passport before you read this book because you will want to hit the road afterwards."
- Chris Christensen, *Amateur Traveler* and *This Week in Travel* podcasts

"Want to know where it's cheap to travel and how do it for less than $100 a day? Then *The World's Cheapest Destinations* is the book for you! Tim Leffel makes me want to pack up my bags because in most of these places it's cheaper than staying home."

- Johnny Jet DiScala, editor of Johnnyjet.com

"There are two ways to travel overseas: You can visit overpriced countries, or you can go to equally exciting destinations on the cheap. Tim Leffel is a master storyteller who graciously informs us on how to maximize our travel experience the inexpensive way. This latest edition updates the best locations worldwide where you can stretch your travel budget to the fullest!"

- Brad Olsen, author of *World Stompers* and *Future Esoteric*

"In Tim's 4th edition of *The World's Cheapest Destinations*, he scoured the world again to help travelers make the most of their travel dollars. Even though I've been studying travel writing and guides for 15+ years, I always learn something new with each edition of Tim's book.

- Sean Keener, CEO of Bootsnall.com

"With a little ingenuity, a bit of creativity and this book, you'll be able to travel many places in the world you never thought possible. *The World's Cheapest Destinations* is hands down the best guide to traveling the world on a budget."

- Beth Whitman, editor of WanderlustAndLipstick.com

"If the size of your travel budget is your starting point (after all, whose isn't?), the practical advice in this updated edition will make it much easier to design an affordable trip. The actual prices quoted look spot on in the countries which I have recently visited."

- Susan Griffith, author of *Work Your Way
Around the World* and *Gap Years for Grown-ups*

"Warning: this book is hazardous to your ability to stay in one place. With your copy of *The World's Cheapest Destinations* in hand, you can see the world while leaving your savings account untouched."

> \- Chris Guillebeau, author of *The $100 Startup*

"This is the book I wish I had before I went traveling. It would have saved me a lot of money and provided better insight on what to expect."

> \- Michael Tieso, editor-in-chief of Art of Backpacking

"It's no fluke that the world's cheapest destinations are often also the most amazing to visit. This valuable guide inadvertently attests that money can't buy happiness by recommending countries where the locals smile without it. "

> – Bruce Northam, author of *The Directions to Happiness: A 125-Country Quest for Life Lessons*

"Buy this before you buy a plane ticket--it's the best first investment for a budget traveler. Leffel provides real numbers and practical money-saving tips, and he wisely weighs the appeal of a country as well. As a result, *The World's Cheapest Destinations* are places you really want to go."

> \- Zora O'Neill, author of *The Rough Guide to Cancun & The Yucatan* and *Moon New Mexico*

"This is the book that anyone planning a vacation should read because it's exactly what travelers who circle the globe all year long already know: it can be really cheap to travel, you just have to know where."

> \- Christine Gilbert, editor of almostfearless.com

"*The World's Cheapest Destinations* is an entertaining read sharing the secrets that long-term travelers and backpackers have known for years. No room for excuses now, with this book you'll have the tools and information you need to travel the world in comfort on a budget. It's an excellent resource for planning and researching your next vacation destination or around-the-world trip and is something that we'll be using regularly for reference whenever we do our own travel planning."

- Deb and Dave, editors of ThePlanetD.com

"A great book if you're on a budget. Even better if you're looking for a more authentic travel experience."

- Peter Moore, author of *No Shitting in the Toilet* and *The Wrong Way Home*

"Tim Leffel has done it again! With this new edition, *The World's Cheapest Destinations* continues to be the most useful, comprehensive book I've ever seen about traveling cheaply. Leffel thoroughly breaks it down for strategic-minded, value-seeking travelers. I recommend this book for shoestring travelers, flashpackers, and glampers alike, or to anyone looking to milk the most from their travels. This book is useful from the very beginning dreaming and planning phases of your upcoming journeys."

- Joshua Berman, author of *Moon Nicaragua* and *Maya 2012: A Guide to Celebrations in Mexico, Guatemala, Belize & Honduras*

For Alina

May her third passport have many stamps.

Table of Contents

Tim Leffel

Introduction

Our tuk-tuk driver had been driving us around the entire day for $14, waiting for us as we explored different sets of ruins. He dropped us at the door of our hotel, where we were paying $44 a night for two connecting rooms with air conditioning, TV, fridge, and a made-to-order huge breakfast. The staffers met us at the door with cool towels and glasses of water, asking us how our day went.

After a warm hot shower in our air-conditioned rooms to wash off the sunscreen and dust, we ventured out to a spa. For two four-hand massages for the adults and a foot massage for the daughter—all lasting an hour—the tab was $26. For dinner we ordered multiple courses from our waiter and had a few rounds of drinks. We paid the $16 tab, did a little shopping at the night market, and then got a tuk-tuk back to our hotel for $2.

On this trip, we were free spenders on a vacation budget. If we were being at all careful with our money, we could have spent far less that day in Siem Reap, Cambodia. On this budget, we were splurging.

Would you like to find out where a $100 a day vacation budget makes you a splurging traveler instead of a tightwad? Would you like to know where tightwads get by on $40 a day...for two? This book will show you, in detail, where to go and why.

This is the fourth edition of *The World's Cheapest Destinations*. The book you are holding (on paper or in pixels) is the best guide you could possibly buy to figure out what countries around the world are the best values. It's also the best investment you could make in putting together a budget for a long-term journey. In short, it will save you both time and money. This is the fourth edition, improved and expanded several times since the first came out in 2003.

If you bought this book and don't gain enough knowledge to save you hundreds or thousands of dollars in your travels, you're either already extremely savvy or you've ignored the advice and spent the summer in Europe instead.

But as I've warned each time before, the world keeps changing, sometimes in a heartbeat.

When we go traveling around the world, we mostly turn off the TV, forget the daily paper, and spend our computer time checking e-mail and keeping in touch more than reading news. The problem is, the world keeps turning and changing and morphing. Revolutions start, currencies crash, and the financial markets create havoc, even when we're on a slacker beach somewhere that doesn't even have electricity. In other words, what was true when we left often won't be true when we're halfway through our trip.

When the last edition of this book came out, there was no "Arab Spring," no economic meltdown in Europe, and no civil war in Syria. The extent of the U.S. housing crisis was just starting to become clear. Who knows what massive changes will strike in the next few years?

Many of the prices that you will read in this book will be a little off or a lot off, due to circumstances far beyond my control. Things I was sure about will be proved wrong. Governments that seemed stable will fall apart and others will suddenly get their act together. As this book went to press, several currencies had fluctuated by 30% or more over the course of six months. So had the price of oil and some food products like corn.

That's reality; get used to it and roll with the punches. The one truism, however, is this: the destinations that are a relative bargain will continue to be a relative bargain over time. Thailand will always be a better value than Japan, Budapest a better deal than Copenhagen. It's just the details that evolve.

When I wrote what became the first edition of *The World's Cheapest Destinations*, the world was a mess. The U.S. stock market was in a tailspin, dragging many other markets around the world down with it. A group of mass murderers had flown commercial jets into the World Trade Center in New York and the Pentagon in Washington, taking thousands of lives—and wrecking thousands of families. A bomb blast in Bali killed 202 people. The U.S. had just invaded Iraq. Several airlines went out of business or went into bankruptcy, and e-mail boxes were flooded with travel deals nobody wanted to take.

Still, back then many people were willing to ignore the bad news and take advantage of the travel bargains. Fortunately for me, a couple thousand even bought my book to find out where they could best stretch their budget. The solid demand for the book surprised a lot of people, including me, so a second edition came out in 2006 when it seemed the popular destinations of the world might buckle under the pressure of an onslaught of new visitors. Prices were rising quickly, especially in Eastern Europe, and hotels were getting away with raising prices every few months.

When the third one came out in 2009, we had come full circle. The world economy was in a funk that was just getting rolling, unemployment passed 10% in the U.S. and Europe, and most of the big legacy airlines had just started on their mission to piss off as many customers as they possibly could. Fuel prices and food prices started bouncing up and down, taking many prices that impact travelers with them.

Are we out of the funk yet? It depends on who you ask. I'm not sure where things will go from here, but no matter what, you will travel well for far less—or travel longer—by being savvy about *where* you travel.

Here are some specifics on what to look out for in the future, regardless of what you read in the individual country chapters to follow.

Prices

In many destinations I featured in earlier editions of this book, prices have barely budged and the estimates are still accurate. Although conditions are more in balance as this book goes to press, that's mostly because the dollar is reasonably strong against the euro and many other currencies. This can turn in a matter of weeks, so keep an eye on international financial news if you want to avoid getting an unpleasant smack on the side of the head upon arrival. Look at this way: in 2008 Iceland briefly became a terrific bargain, while in 2011, Brazil's capital was listed as one of the most expensive cities in the world to live. When currencies get out of balance, anything can happen. Eventually, equilibrium usually takes over and the cheapest stay cheapest relative to others on the continent.

The divergent paths of the world's currency markets make my job especially difficult, as this is meant to be a book with global appeal. I've kept all prices in U.S. dollars, which is still the easiest currency to change almost anywhere in the world (though euros are the number one choice in a few non-European spots), so you'll have to do a quick calculation if your travel budget is in another currency. Unless the dollar and euro get back to parity, it's safe to say that western Europeans will keep finding amazing bargains around the world for a while. If you live in a country whose currency closely tracks the euro, don't stay home waiting it to go back up 10% against the dollar. Get on a plane!

As this book went to press, Canadian and Australian dollars were close to par with the U.S. one, so you won't have to do any math if that's your own currency. Much of the strength in those two is due to high commodity prices, especially oil and gold, so that could change in the coming years.

Prices around the world will change no matter what and they're usually more likely to go up than down. For one thing, fuel prices have become very volatile, so rates for a plane ticket, taxi, bus, banana, or loaf of bread will go up accordingly. A rising global population, China's growing thirst for energy, and global warming's impact on weather/crops are all factors that aren't going away. The ripple effect of rising fuel and food prices is a wild card that will cause riots, bankruptcies, and yes, an uncertain climate for travelers.

Country Changes

When choosing the countries to be included in the first edition, I kept it simple. My criteria were that places had to be cheap, there had to be at least some semblance of a tourist infrastructure, and destinations had to attract more than a handful of travelers—or had the potential to very soon. So while some countries scored high on the "cheap" criteria, they often failed on the second two.

I loosened up a bit on the second edition to add some "honorable mentions" for each continent. I added information on the countries in East Africa that make up a well-worn backpacker trail in the region. I still think Africa is a tough trip to do on a budget because of the costs of a decent safari, the expensive flight prices, and the local transportation costs, but I'll leave that up to you to decide.

There are two country changes in this edition: I moved Argentina to the "honorable mentions" section for the Americas and added a full Cambodia chapter to the Asia section. The former has gotten too pricey for its own section in this book, while cheap Cambodia has greatly improved its tourism infrastructure (especially roads and buses) lately. I also moved Turkey to the honorable mentions for Europe and replaced it with Slovakia.

Hey, You Missed a Spot!

There are notable omissions in this book, including plenty of places where you could travel around for less than $20 a day if you took local buses and ate where the locals eat. I have my reasons though. Cheap destinations that are in war zones, or are just really sad places to travel through on a day-to-day basis aren't here. Even the most fearless traveler will admit that some places just aren't worth the risk or the depression.

Some third world destinations offer cheap grub and accommodations, but little of interest for people who aren't missionaries or Peace Corps workers. Unless you just plan on smoking dope and watching the donkeys stroll by, you'll be starved for something to do. Many of these countries are also a royal pain to get around unless you have your own vehicle (and plenty of cash for roadblock bribes).

Some destinations are only mentioned in passing because frankly, their neighbors have much more to offer for the price or the political situation makes it not worth the trouble. There are good reasons why Iran's visitor numbers are a fraction of Jordan's, or why Paraguay's are a fraction of Ecuador's, or why you don't see a lot of guidebooks for Moldova. Still other countries are tucked away in some remote corner of the world; you'll have the thrill of discovering those all on your own. Hopefully the destinations listed here provide a wide enough range for everyone. My goal is to give an overview on the best values around the world so you can pick and choose what works best for your situation.

Now get outta' town!

No rules. Instant fares.

Get an instant price to visit the world's cheapest destinations.

GLOBAL TRIP PLANNER

indie.bootsnall.com

It's Not How You Go, but Where!

Yes, traveling overseas can be expensive, but it sure doesn't have to be. The key to living it up abroad is not related to airline specials, discount hotel vouchers, or finding the cheapest restaurant in Rome or Paris. The way to really travel well without spending your life savings is to go to where your first world dollars, euros, or pounds are worth a fortune.

A taxi ride from the airport to the center of town is around $10 in Quito and $15 in Kuala Lumpur, but can hit $120 in Milan and $180 in Tokyo. For the price of a bed in a tiny dorm in Tokyo or Venice, you can get a beautiful double room in a hotel with a pool in many parts of Southeast Asia. For the price of simple dinner for two in Western Europe, you could pig out for a whole week in Indonesia, Nepal, or India. For the $9 you'd pay for one beer in a bar in Oslo, you could buy a round of beers for yourself and a large table of friends in Granada (Nicaragua), Sofia, Saigon, or Brno.

Even neighboring countries can have drastically different prices. When I crossed from Bolivia to Chile in 2012, beers went from $1 to $4, basic hotels went from $30 to $90, taxi prices quadrupled, and even going to the public bathroom went from 14¢ to 60¢. The only thing I could find that hadn't gone up drastically was Chilean wine.

Most travel books and articles won't tell you that. They'll tell you things such as how to shave $40 off the price of a flight, how to find promotional hotel deals, or how you can save 25% on European trains by booking in advance. Guidebooks will tell you what a certain country or region will cost, but they seldom compare those costs to other destinations. Even by scouring the Web for days on end, you'd be hard pressed to find any resource that will tell you where the cheapest countries are and which places offer the best value.

While all the practical advice on budgeting and finding a good deal is useful, it doesn't help so much if the destination is expensive to start with. If you're worried about money the whole time you're traveling or are thinking about how much your dinner is setting you back while you're eating it, you're probably not enjoying the experience very much. A $60 "bargain" meal in Paris is still $60, which could feed you for a week in the many of the countries featured here—or get you a romantic candlelight dinner for two in the best restaurant in town.

How much will I spend?

Estimating travel costs is difficult since there are a lot of variables to consider: how much you are moving around, what class of transportation you are taking, and even how much you eat. In general, a couple can travel around the countries in this book for $850 to $1,700 a month at the budget end, or anywhere from $1,000 to $3,000 a month staying in mid-range hotels and taking the best available ground transportation. Most solo backpackers can travel around the world for $750 to $1,500 a month after airfare, gear purchases, and inoculations before you go. Again, it depends a lot of how much you're moving around and where you spend the night.

Compare that to what you normally spend for a one-week vacation at some beach resort or in Paris—or even what you spend just to pay your regular bills at home. Some homeowner travelers I have met in my journeys were renting out their house or condo while they were traveling and were spending less than the profit that was coming in! Renters who put their things in storage often marveled at how they had cut their expenses in half, but were out seeing the world instead of doing the same thing every week.

Your mileage will vary of course. A few years back I got reports from two couples who recently returned from yearlong round-the-world trips. One couple was frugal and spent around $14,000, including flights. The other couple left with loads of cash in the bank and spent $85,000. Obviously they were traveling in different styles, but the first couple visited 11 countries and moved relatively slowly. The other couple was on a whirlwind tour and landed in 40 different countries. Each couple had different priorities, a different level of comfort, and different goals—plus more time in Europe in the latter case.

There are several ironies that work in your favor when you travel on the cheap though. First, many of the world's most awe-inspiring sights are located in the world's cheapest countries. Think of all the great man-made monuments: The Taj Mahal, the Great Pyramids, Machu Picchu, Petra, Borobudur, Aya Sofia, Ankor Wat, Tikal, and all the Roman ruins scattered outside Rome. Or if you prefer natural wonders, you can explore the most unspoiled rain forests, go white water rafting on raging rivers, hike up volcanoes, kayak around some of the world's prettiest beaches, or go trekking in the Himalayas (just to name a few).

Second, the less money you spend in any given location, the more likely you are to interact with the people who actually live there instead of just other tourists. You'll also get much better deals on everything than your "Europe in Seven Days" counterparts. These vacationers seal themselves in familiar chain hotels, travel in packs, and do everything in a hurry, including their shopping. With a little bit of effort, you can spend a fraction of what they do and have a better time as well.

If you visit the destinations listed in this guide, you'll eat great meals, experience mind-blowing things, meet people you'll never forget, and come back with photos that'll amaze your friends and family—probably for less than you spend each month just to put a roof over your head. If you work, volunteer, or study abroad, you'll spend even less and get the education of a lifetime.

The V.F.A.Q. (Very Frequently Asked Questions)
I've been to more countries than I can keep track of at this point and have talked with hundreds of travelers that have been to others I missed. Nearly anyone who travels to distant, exotic lands can expect the following questions from curious relatives and friends, especially if they're American or Canadian. (Unlike the citizens of most other developed countries, we tend to have little vacation time to really travel).

3

I'm guessing you may have some of the same questions yourself:

1) Don't you have to learn the local language?
I have a theory that the main reason so many Australians and Americans go to England on vacation is because people there speak English. There's this fear of not being able to communicate in places where English isn't the first language.

In some places it helps a great deal to know a second language, especially Latin America, China, and parts of Eastern Europe. In others (like Thailand or Malaysia) it's barely worth trying unless you're going to put down roots. In India and Nepal, anyone who has been to school speaks English.

Outside the latter two, however, a phrase book should stay in your pocket, especially if you'll be in rural areas or eating in working-class eateries. Learning a bit of the local language will certainly enhance your experience if you'll be in one country for a while. If you'll be in Latin America it's worth learning some Spanish; you can use it from Mexico all the way down to the bottom of Chile and Argentina. You'll also get ripped off less if you learn the local numbers and how to bargain. Among the educated, the business people, and those who depend on tourists for a living, however, English rules.

2) How can you afford to travel for so long?
I used to get this question all the time when I would go away and not come back for a year. Now I go away for three weeks and people still ask the same question.

Tell someone you're going overseas for a few weeks to a year and they automatically think you've gotten an inheritance or an overseas job. The latter is a great experience, but not necessary for anyone with a bit of savings.

The airfare can be a big expense, but after that you can stretch your dollars a long way. Some backpackers go for months on a few grand and in some places you'd have to try really hard to spend over $40 a day. During my three-week

Himalayan trek in Nepal, for example, I spent a total of $180, despite eating my fill and having a real bed to sleep on each night. If I'd hired a private porter for the whole trip and spent as much as I possibly could, I might have been able to bump that budget up to $360. Now, 15 years later, you can still easily do it for less than $600, half that if you carry your own pack.

Now that I'm not a vagabonding backpacker, I routinely take more comfortable international vacations of two or three weeks with my wife, and sometimes with my daughter as well. We always spend less than a visitor to Western Europe or Japan does in just a few days. Costs mostly depend on where you go.

Budgeting for travel also depends on how you handle your personal finances, of course. I find that most people who ask how I can afford to travel so much are the same people who are in debt up to their eyeballs and are always driving a brand new car—or two. For the price of a MacBook or the best iPad, you can spend two or weeks or more traversing almost any country in this book. I've got friends who spend more on their McMansion mortgage in one month, than I spend on a three-week family vacation. If you can't afford to travel, take a hard look at where the rest of your money is going and decide what's important. You can easily travel to most anywhere in the world if you're making a decent living, but not if all your earnings are just going into paying for more stuff.

3) Isn't it really dangerous in _____?

You can find danger anywhere if you go looking for it, but nearly every stat you look at shows that the world is becoming a safer place. The number of travelers hurt by something other than their own stupidity is amazingly small considering the millions on the move each week. If you're the type that freaks out easily, your best bet is to turn off the TV and get your news from better sources.

Every year since I started putting out this book there have been natural and manmade disasters. There will continue to be major floods, hurricanes, typhoons, tornadoes, mudslides, forest fires, bombings, plane crashes, train crashes, and more. Most of these do not affect travelers; they strike homes, commuter lines, and neighborhoods from Japan to New York City to Australia.

It has been safer in any given year to be some places rather than others, but not if you happened to live and work where the trouble was. And "where the trouble was" could not accurately be predicted on any risk map. One year, Athens is risky and Mexico City is not. The next year things reverse or the new trouble spot is wherever the latest bomb blast or flood occurred.

Much of the random risk is purely accidental, while in other cases it's equally random acts of violence. Muslim terrorists are continuing to do what they do best: kill innocent people in cruel and unpredictable ways, in unpredictable places. One year, Spain and England, another year India and the Philippines. Next year, who knows?

You could be forgiven for wanting to lock the doors and curl up on the sofa with a bag of cheese curls and a bowl of ice cream. But don't forget, fewer people died from all of last year's disasters, bombings, and plane crashes than die from heart disease each year. Your odds of dying in an airplane crash are one in 659,779 (about the same odds as being dealt a royal flush in 5-card stud poker). Your odds of dying in a car wreck are one in 6,585. Your odds of dying from heart disease are one in 388. More people die each year from slipping and falling in their bathtub than from terrorist attacks. (But moms, you should really chill out at the playground: the odds of your child dying in a fall there are 1 in 299,400,000—about the same as dying from a scorpion sting if you're also worried about that.)

The lesson? Put away the snacks, garage the car, and go eat some rice and vegetables in Asia.

When it comes to crime, chances are no matter where you're going, the evening news is not as scary as it is in your own hometown. The U.S. has one of the highest crime rates on Earth, ranking 88 out of 158 nations in the Global Peace Index. Thuggery is rampant in England and Canada's stats would surely be higher if an estimated 50% of its property crimes didn't go unreported. The worst places for pickpockets are Lisbon and Rome—not exactly tourist backwaters. Americans alone take over 80 million international trips each year and a miniscule fraction experience real crime. Apart from visiting the war zones of the world, you're as likely to suffer harm in your own neighborhood or driving to work than you are by traveling overseas.

Yes, you need to keep your wits about you, avoid scams, and don't make it easy for pickpockets. Learn which cities and regions to avoid or get in and out of quickly (Mexican border towns, most of Pakistan, Caracas, the Moskito Coast, and any place with the word "Congo" or "Sudan" in it for a start). Don't walk around decked out in Rolex and Prada, despite what you see on the pages of *Travel & Leisure*. In some spots it's often better to look a bit grubby rather than filthy rich. Also, read news from an overseas source and find out what's going on locally. Surf the travel message boards to confirm the real situation on the ground. Crime usually occurs in predictable places and rarely impacts tourists. In other cases, you need to exercise extra caution.

In more than 20 years of regular international travel, however, the only significant problems I have suffered are two stolen cameras—and one of those was stolen by another traveler. (Plus we think a hotel maid stole a watch of my wife's, but it was at a five-star hotel when I was on assignment.) This includes three months in Indonesia during Suharto's downfall and watching a riot from my hotel balcony in northern India. Most people I know have done worse at home.

4) How do you set all this up ahead of time?

The easy answer is, "Don't." If you build in the opportunity for surprise, your travels will be far more interesting than if everything is mapped out to the hour. When my wife and I backpacked around the world for years in the pre-Internet days, we only made reservations when it was absolutely necessary. In close to 1,000 nights of lodging, there was only been one night we couldn't find a room (so we took a bus to the next town). Three or four times we had to suck it up and pay for a more expensive room than we expected. This generally only happens if there's a local festival or a national holiday, you're in Europe during the summer, or if you're in an area where there's only one hotel.

The "Europe in the summer" part has been a drastic change in the past decade. Despite the high prices there, the continent is packed from June through August, especially in the capital cities. Plan on mapping out an itinerary and sticking to it, reserving hostel beds in advance—or going somewhere else you can be more spontaneous.

In other locations, make a reservation for the night you'll get off the plane. Read a guidebook and find out if there's a crunch for rooms in certain towns. Otherwise, be aware of what's going on locally and you'll be fine. Tens of thousands of people are traveling this way right now as you read this book.

If it is high season or you just want some peace of mind, however, you can do almost anything in advance over the Internet. You will pay a bit more sometimes, but then you can go on vacation without worrying about where you're staying or where to pick up train tickets. You can book hostel beds, pick out a small inn, rent a car, hire a driver, or get a bus schedule, all from the comfort of your computer chair. Travel is easy now. Take advantage of it. Just don't let this get in the way of serendipity and following the road where it takes you. Any experienced traveler will tell you the most interesting adventures came out of unplanned side trips and encounters.

5) What's it going to cost ME?

Only you can answer this question really. It depends on how you travel, if you're traveling with someone else, and how much discomfort you're willing to endure.

Airfare is a big cost, but the plethora of budget airlines on many continents makes it fairly cheap once you cross an ocean. The costs of getting around are covered in the individual country chapters. Many of the countries featured in this book are clustered together in regions where you can go from one to the other overland, by bus or train. In these cases the costs of moving on will be minimal.

Take all estimates on daily expenses presented in this book as a *very* rough guideline; a lot of it depends on your personal comfort level. Some backpackers will spend $10 a day in southern India and consider themselves to be living better than they do at home. After all, they're being waited on for three meals a day in restaurants. No dishes to wash. Others may spend $250 each a day and complain that the TV doesn't get CNN.

I've tried to provide a wide enough margin to accommodate for this and to give two ranges. The backpackers budget is for those who use basic rooms with a fan, take a lot of local transport, walk a lot, and eat where the locals do a good bit of the time, especially outside Southeast Asia. In some places they'll use a communal kitchen and buy groceries. For the countries in this book, $850 to $1,700 per month for two backpackers (after airfare) should cover it.

The mid-range budget considers nicer rooms with a private bath and A/C where it makes sense, restaurants that are a step up from the bottom tier, and tourist buses or better train classes in most areas. This varies widely by country. It could be as little as $750 for a whole month in Nepal and parts of Indonesia, or as high as a few thousand dollars in Peru, Morocco, or Hungary if seeing all there is to see, doing all there is to do.

Of course there's a lot of overlap; most backpackers will splurge now and then on things that give them pleasure and most mid-range travelers will sleep in a $5 bamboo beach bungalow if it's clean and in a nice location. Some people are backpackers where it's more expensive and turn into mid-range travelers when they get to a place like Indonesia, where the difference between a hovel and a palace can be a dollar or two.

How much you're moving around will have a big impact on expenses. Hitting all the highlights of a country on a two-week vacation is going to cost far more than two weeks of swinging in a hammock on a secluded beach somewhere. If you're one of those nuts trying to tick off 30+ countries in 12 months, double the budgets you read in here; you'll be handing much of your savings over to transportation operators.

Note that a person traveling alone will spend more than a person sharing rooms with someone else will. I've referred to two people as a "couple" in this book, but that can be two friends who have arrived together or just two people that met up and are traveling together to save on expenses. A couple can usually travel on roughly 1.5 times what a single person can, due to room shares, taxi shares, and splitting some meal items. It's also safer at times and makes for better bargaining; there's strength in numbers. So if a single person averages $20 a day, a couple will probably average $30 a day for the same experience. Being a loner has plenty of advantages, but few financial ones. (A couple traveling together can also lighten their load by carrying one of many items between them, such as a deck of cards, a medical kit, or a flashlight.)

Some hard-core shoestring travelers will surely read my estimates in these destination chapters and say, "I spent less than that." Well, good for you, but this isn't a contest. Those who scrape by on the barest of budgets are usually the ones skipping museums, major sites, and most side trip adventures that are not free or cheap. But going all the way to Peru and skipping Machu Picchu, or being in Jordan and skipping Petra is just idiotic. Yes, you'll spend more than a day's budget, but it won't be an ordinary day. Ten years from now, are you really going to be happy you didn't spend that extra $42 or even $100? Or are you going to be glad you didn't go white-water rafting somewhere because it allowed you to travel an extra day or two in the end?

It's much better to travel for a month and take advantage of everything a destination has to offer than to travel for two and be broke all the time. This doesn't mean spending foolishly; it means having enough to do and see what's worth doing and seeing. The reason to go to the countries in this book is you can do all that on a tiny fraction of what it costs at home.

I've only mentioned first-class travel in passing here and there, mainly when a top-class train is a great value or spending money on a top hotel is a special experience. Traveling first-class in these countries is cheaper than traveling first-class in Western Europe or Japan, but not by much. There are impressive resorts in Thailand that charge $2,000 per night and there's a lovely one-day train trip in Peru that's $600 per person. Although it boggles my mind, there are hotels in India with nightly rates listed as "starting at $850." In India! If you want, you can go to Nepal on a guided tour that's $450 each per day—although I think you're tossing your money away to do so. So if you demand pampering at every stage, you will pay pampering prices, no matter where you are. This book isn't much help at that level.

On the same note, the prices in this book are most applicable to destinations within the countries where locals are at least as plentiful as tourists. Even in the cheapest countries, there are resort areas built to accommodate fat tourists with fat wallets: places like Cancun and Cabo San Lucas in Mexico, Agadir in Morocco, Sharm-el-Sheik in Egypt, and Kemer (near Antalya) in Turkey. Avoid these spots unless you are hankering for a place just like home—with rates to match.

All prices in this book are quoted in U.S. dollars. That's not me being an ugly American—it's still the reality of the global marketplace. The euro is definitely favored in some spots and you can cash that currency in more places all the time, but dollars can be exchanged nearly everywhere on the globe—just carry crisp new bills when possible as Ben Franklin is the counterfeiters' favorite face to copy.

Except where mentioned, I didn't include student prices in this book; better to get a surprise to the upside and pay less. If you're a student with the right ID—or have purchased the right ID in Bangkok (ahem)—then assume you'll pay less than what I've posted for museums and government-run transportation options such as trains.

6) *What's the Catch?*

"If it sounds too good to be true, it probably is" the saying goes. Another saying is, "everything in life is a trade-off," which is probably more apt for this situation. In essence, these countries are cheap because they're not nearly as rich as first-world nations such as Japan, the U.S., Canada, and most of Western Europe. If you leave your home country with $10,000 in the bank, you are already better off than 67% of the entire world's population. The wealth you see around you at home is abnormal—it's not how most of the world lives.

As a result, at times you'll surely encounter inept and corrupt government officials, you'll find that departure times are rarely more than rough estimates, you often can't drink the tap water, and you certainly won't have the vast choices and conveniences you're used to at home. You'll also find scary bathrooms at times. You may need shots to prevent scarier diseases. You'll probably find the idea of renting a car and playing chicken with the local highway drivers to be a bit *too* adventurous.

Each negative usually has a corresponding positive, however. You won't find miles of bland strip malls and parking lots. You'll be forced to try new food and customs, some of which you'll end up really liking. You'll learn something about other religions and traditions that doesn't come from a textbook or a news sound bite. You'll read and hear news with a whole different perspective. And you'll see your own country through others' eyes—something it wouldn't hurt our elected leaders to do once in a while.

Last, you'll appreciate what you have more and realize that most of the world's people lead happy lives having just a fraction of what we spend our money on. Even as a backpacker, you'll spend more freely than they can dream of spending, so you might feel downright rich for the first time in your life.

7) Can you do this with kids?

I haven't made any notes about traveling with little children in the chapters. I have a daughter and I have taken her abroad to eight countries now, but I am not yet ready to take her on crappy third-world buses, pumping her full of malaria pills, exposing her to aggressive deformed beggars, or trying to ward off touts while simultaneously keeping her occupied. Not to mention what would have ended up in her mouth when she was a toddler!

But that's just me. Plenty of people feel differently and they have no qualms about taking their baby or toddler on dusty packed buses in India or Mozambique. At the least, adjust. Don't travel like the childless people travel. Slow down your pace, narrow your geography, and bring enough money to ensure some safety and privacy. You may think your kids are precious, but people on the other side of a thin-walled backpacker hotel will not, especially when your kids are making noise at 7:00 a.m—just a few hours after your hotel mates went to bed. Trust me on this one. It doesn't mean you have to avoid reasonably priced hotels, just find ones that are kid-friendly or are spread out enough to give you some space.

There are some good books out there on traveling with children that aren't all about Disney and Hawaii. See the resources section on the accompanying website to this book: www.worldscheapestdestinations.com

Once your children are old enough and adjusted enough to know which way the wind blows, you should be able to take kids to any of these places and have a good time.

8) What's it like for vegetarians?

Where applicable, I've tried to address what the situation is like for vegetarians or those who only eat seafood. My wife fit this category for a decade-and-a-half, so I know how tough it can be at times. In some places (mostly in Asia) it's no sweat, and in India and Nepal being a vegetarian is standard practice. In others places it means very limited choices or some form of bread, rice, beans, or cheese.

If you're currently a strict vegan, you'll probably need to change your eating habits in many places. Otherwise, carry a portable stove or forget eating hot meals. Restaurants in many of these countries are so cheap that virtually no budget hotels have kitchens. You'll have trouble straying from the "gringo trails" of the world, but in those spots it will be easy if you're not on the lowest of low budgets. There are some good books and resources out there though, which I've listed on WorldsCheapestDestinations.com.

Understand that in nearly all developing countries outside the Indian subcontinent, being a vegetarian means you can't afford to buy meat. It's beyond the locals' comprehension that you would forgo it on purpose.

9) *What's it like for gay and lesbian travelers?*

I haven't addressed the situation for gay and lesbian travelers at all in the individual chapters, but I've provided some good resources on the website and most guidebooks now give a good sense of the scene. In general, it's easier for women everywhere, and easier for men in Asia. In parts of the Middle East, friends of the same sex commonly walk down the street holding hands. Latin America and parts of Eastern Europe can be tough, though every country has its scene; the difference is how underground you need to go. In Buenos Aires or Mexico City, it's a dream. In Cairo, it's a different story.

Simply being discreet will avoid a lot of problems. In most countries profiled here, modesty rules. Even married couples will attract a lot of attention if they're overly public with their affections. Conversely, there are plenty of people sharing a room with someone of the same sex for economic reasons, so you won't attract attention simply by traveling together and sleeping in the same bed.

Next Steps

This book is meant to be a primer, an overview, and a jumping-off point. It can't possibly take the place of a thick, general travel advice guide, or a guidebook for a specific destination or region. You'll still need those once you decide what destinations sound appealing. What this book will do is provide a little flavor of the destination, give you an idea how much you'll spend there, and help you get a feel for where you'd like to go.

If this book gets you excited enough to go somewhere that's featured, do your homework before you leave. Figure out if there's a bad time for weather. Figure out how much you can reasonably see in the time you've set aside and leave plenty of wiggle room. Read lots of advice on what to pack and what to do. If you don't, you'll be one of those clueless tourists everyone else will be making fun of when you're not looking. ("Gosh, I had no idea it was so rainy this time of year!")

If you're going for more than two weeks, make sure you've taken care of what happens to any bills and mail while you're gone. Figure out whether your credit or debit card will work where you're going and how you'll stash enough money to deal with rural areas.   I've listed lots of resources on the website, but the Lonely Planet message board has the best forum out there for asking other travelers for advice. Here's a book I co-wrote that's centered on one area, but is a gold mine for preparation info: *Traveler's Tool Kit: Mexico and Central America.* For general advice on getting the most out of your budget in any location, see my other book, *Make Your Travel Dollars Worth a Fortune.*

I've addressed visas in a few spots, but this is fluid and you'll need to research this aspect as well. In many countries, Americans, Brits, and Canadians don't need one at all, but in other parts of the world you could shell out $130 or more for a visa that's only good for a limited period. Some visas you can get upon arrival just for coughing up the cash, but in others it takes several days or more for a background check. Some countries, like Argentina and Bolivia, will sock you with the same amount your own government charges, so that can put a huge dent in your budget. Be prepared.

This book should give you a good overview of the world's best travel deals for anyone traveling on a sub-luxury budget.

On the World's Cheapest Destinations website you'll find places to go for more detailed information, including where to go to find some of the best sources on each topic. My blog is a great resource too, with more than 1,000 posts on traveling well for less.

Stop dreaming, start reading, and begin planning—it's cheaper and easier than you think!

ASIA

For long-term travelers setting out from most parts of the world, Asia—especially Southeast Asia—is nearly always on the list. Lonely Planet's first guidebook was *Southeast Asia on a Shoestring* and the region still seems to attract an inordinate number of the world's backpackers.

We can argue for a while about which country in the world is the best value for travelers, but if you had to pick the top five, the majority would be in Asia.

If you're American, and to a lesser extent Canadian, you aren't likely to meet all that many people from your home country, however. Instead you'll be sharing the road with residents of Europe, Australia, New Zealand, and Japan. Lately, a fair number of Korean and Chinese people as well. For the most part, this is a matter of geography and flight prices. It's much easier for North Americans to sit on a four-hour plane ride to Central America and be in the same time zone than it is to sit on a 15- or 20-hour flight to Thailand and be dragging for two days. Australians can fly to Bali like East Coast Americans fly to the Bahamas, but a trip from North America to Asia is not an easy thing to fit into a short vacation.

Flight prices to Asia have kept rising as fuel costs have gone up. This is a good place to cash in frequent flier miles if you've been banking some. Sometimes the best bet is to visit several countries with an around-the-world or circle-the-Pacific flight package (most of the latter are $1,500 to $4,000). Otherwise, your round trip flight will likely cost several hundred dollars more than one to the bottom of South America or Eastern Europe, or at least double the cost from the U.S. to Central America. In the weird world of vacation packages, it is often cheaper to buy a package trip to these Asian countries, with hotel rooms included, than it is to buy a flight by itself. This is especially true for Europeans.

Once you get here, however, you'll live very well for very little money and you can get around for cheap. In most of these countries, you can still find $5 cheapie hotel rooms, splashed-

17

out rooms with the works for $25, and very cheap local transportation that's sometimes even comfortable. You can get a healthy meal for a dollar or two. Except for a few major historic sites, you won't pay much to go sightseeing either. You'll find souvenir prices that are too low to believe. In other words, you can do it all without having to cut back somewhere. If you are a vacationing couple budgeting $100 or $200 a day, you can really live it up and come home with money to spare.

In most of the Asian countries included here, a backpacking couple can get by on $30-$60 a day with just a little effort. For $50 per day per person, you can pretty much stop thinking about money if you're traveling like a backpacker, but not on the move every day, especially in the bottom destinations mentioned earlier. This is not to say your comfort level will be consistent, however. Thailand, Vietnam, and Malaysia run like well-oiled machines, while you may find it a wonder that India runs at all. You'll take more than your share of cold showers and in Indonesia that might mean pouring a bucket of water over your head.

Unless you're well off the beaten track, however, you can generally spend a couple more dollars and increase your standard of living quite easily: this amount is often the difference between a third and second-class train, between a hard seat and a sleeping berth, or between a crummy bus and a luxury one. Five dollars more a night for your beach accommodations can be the difference between a cramped hut and a big beachfront bungalow. In a city, $5 a night can be the difference in a fan-cooled cubicle with shared bath and an air-conditioned room with a hot shower and maid service.

Mid-range travelers can really feel rich in much of Asia, enjoying a royal lifestyle on what would be a campground budget at home.

It's hard to make many generalizations about Asia, but there are a few. First, everyone gets up very early, often before sunrise. If you want to sleep late, you'll need to choose your room locations carefully or opt for air conditioning to drown out the noise.

Second, large Asian cities in underdeveloped countries are nearly always congested, noisy, and unbelievably polluted. I've noted the few that are pleasant in the coming chapters. Except in those cases, you'll probably want to do a day or two of sightseeing, get your necessary business done, and move out to calmer areas. Third, it's so cheap to eat out that hardly any hotels have kitchens. If you have strict dietary requirements, you'll need to lug along a mini camp stove and a pot, and one of those cards that explains your situation in the local language.

The countries included for Asia are the same except in this fourth edition of the book, Cambodia got a promotion: it has its own chapter now instead of being an "honorable mention." With dramatic improvement in its roads, its safety situation, and its tourism infrastructure, Cambodia has gone from basket case to bucket list status in less than a decade. It's a terrific bargain.

ASIA

Thailand

It's fitting that this book starts with Thailand, because it seems like most of the world's backpackers have spent time here. Bangkok's Khao San Road is the kind of street where you can run into the same travelers three or four times over the course of several months, even though you've never met. Bangkok is the undisputed center for bargain flights to nearly any destination and it's an easy place to apply for visas, so it serves as a travelers' crossroads.

However, Thailand is a favorite for value-seeking travelers of all budgets. Some of the world's best luxury hotel rooms are surprisingly cheap. Where else in the world can you routinely find hotels that make travel magazine top-10 lists going for under $250 per night? Of course you *can* spend more if you want. At exotic beach resorts with names like Amanpuri, Andara, and Trisara, rooms start at more than $700 per night.

At the other end, it's easy to find a room nearly anywhere in the country for 250 baht—around $8. The country's currency, at a shade above 30 to the dollar when I wrote this, tends to bounce around a lot depending on economic and political factors. So expect the prices listed here to fluctuate depending on what's going on in the currency markets. The one thing that hasn't changed is the steady rise in the number of tourists. This is no exotic backwater; Thailand now gets around 16 million visitors a year. This is despite hurdles that would kill the popularity of a lesser country: regular coups, protests that shut down the airport for days, natural disasters, and scuffles with secession-minded Muslims near the southern border.

The country would probably be popular even without the bargain prices. Beautiful beaches, fantastic sights, an array of adventurous activities, and great food are all a strong draw. Besides, transportation here is a breeze.

By backpacker standards, everything is a breeze in Thailand. They've had plenty of practice hosting budget travelers, so you're never at a loss to find what you need and there's nearly always someone around that speaks enough English to help you. Tourism has altered attitudes (and produced lots of scammers) in the "land of smiles," people are generally friendly, especially when you get out of congested, traffic-choked Bangkok.

You don't need a visa to enter for most nationalities, but be advised that you can only stay for 15 days if arriving overland or 30 days if arriving by air. It's much harder than it used to be to stay on continuously by just doing lots of visa runs to neighboring countries. Applying in advance in your home country you can get a 60-day visa in advance, which is plenty for most tourists. If you're going to stick around and teach English or try to work in some other way, you'll probably need to go through the right channels to get a lengthier stay.

Plenty of airlines use Bangkok as a hub, so you can get there and away easily and relatively cheaply, no matter what your itinerary is like. The legacy carriers have been joined by a wide array of budget airlines serving destinations within the country and close by. You can also travel by train or bus to Laos, Myanmar (Burma), Malaysia, Cambodia, and Singapore.

Two can still travel fairly easily here on $35-$70 per day if staying in cheap guesthouses and eating where locals do, especially if you are in one place for a while before moving on to the next spot. Prices don't vary a whole lot throughout the country, although rural areas tend to be a bit cheaper, especially in the northeast. The living is cheap and easy on the more secluded beaches, but those get harder to find each year. It seems like every beach is creeping upmarket and if you head to the popular party island of Koh Pha-Ngan, be prepared to pay inflated prices. It's hard to even find a room at all during the Full Moon parties there, no matter what you are willing to pay. Arrive a week early to lock it in. Prices in Phuket and other resort areas are geared mostly to package vacationers, although the deals there are good if your budget is geared to a vacation rather than long-term travel.

It's hard to stick to a budget here because there are a lot of temptations, from adventure activities to nightlife to great food. If you like to party, that will drive your costs up significantly: Thailand is not a country where you can drink for cheap. (Hold off until Cambodia and Vietnam for that.)

Sightseeing highlights include the old ruins of Ayutthaya, Lop Buri, and Sukothai, plus some stunning architectural sights in Bangkok. There are some zoo-like hill tribe hiking opportunities in the north (Laos and Vietnam are more authentic) and jungle hikes in the national parks. Most people end up heading for the beaches eventually, where you can kayak, snorkel, scuba dive, or just kick back and relax.

Overall, Thailand keeps pulling in the visitors because it offers an incredible variety of attractions, great food, worthwhile shopping, and prices that are easy to swallow. There is a distinct Buddhist culture and a wide array of things to do, from "hitting the sights" to just doing nothing. With a solid infrastructure and generally good service at all budget levels, it's hard to go wrong here.

Accommodation:

The average price for a guesthouse: double room with shared bath or beach bungalow with ceiling fan and private bath is $7 to $14, which is not all that much higher than rooms were going for a decade ago, before SARS, Avian Bird Flu, a tsunami, and a few riots. You can occasionally find a remote hut with a shared bath for as little as 150 baht for two (around $5), though they're getting rare. Ten dollars is a more reasonable bottom, especially at popular beaches. Spending a few dollars more can result in a much nicer room, or a beachfront bungalow with hammock, as opposed to a cramped hut further back from the shore.

In Bangkok, some of the cheapie "rooms" are usually little more than sectioned-off cubicles, but outside the city you'll have more privacy. Many guesthouses have a common hangout area or restaurant on the first floor.

A hotel with TV, A/C, and hot shower can be found for as little as $20, even in Bangkok, $25 to $50 is more common. For $15 to $30, double on some islands, you can get a gorgeous bungalow with a veranda and a drop-dead view.

Nice 3-star rooms with mini-bar, room service, a hotel pool, etc. start at around $35 and most four-star hotels are routinely on offer for under $100 per night. Some of these are all-suite hotels and most include breakfast. International chains like Sheraton and Sofitel frequently list rates under $150 in Bangkok and Chiang Mai, and go for even less on Hotwire. Rates seldom top $300 for a standard double, even at world-famous hotels that routinely place high in travel magazine readers' polls. Exceptions are the truly high-end luxury palaces from the likes of Banyan Tree and Four Seasons.

Bangkok, Chiang Mai, and Phuket are always overstocked with rooms at the mid and upper levels, so competition for guests with money is fierce. Always shop around or bargain for a better rate!

If you're a family of three or more, you might have to shop a little harder for a suitable room: many listed as having two beds just have two twins. In some cases it can make sense to get an apartment instead, either for a week through the normal vacation rental services or for a shorter term through sites like Wimdu.com. We got a nice two-bedroom apartment on the Skytrain line in Bangkok for $60 a night including fees. This was only slightly more than the $45 to $55 we'd been averaging for hotels.

If you want to put down roots for a while, you can rent a house for under $150 a month in rural areas up north, or build a house for as little as $20 per square foot. You'll need a residency permit, which is pretty tough to manage without work sponsorship or a Thai spouse. Condos are easier to buy as a foreigner and are more in the $50 to $150 per square foot range.

Food & Drink:

All those great Thai dishes you're used to sampling at home for $10 a plate and up are on offer here for next to nothing. Coconut curries, pad thais, big noodle soups, and the like run 75¢ to $2 on the street, $1 to $4 in simple restaurants, even with seafood. The variety is excellent, the quality is uniformly high, and even most street stalls are extremely clean and sanitary—just don't drink the tap water. Bottled water is 20¢ to 40¢ a liter; sodas are 40¢ to 80¢. You will drink four or five liters of water a day and sweat most of it back out, however, so for the sake of your budget and the environment, it's worth investing in a SteriPen to purify regular tap water. My whole family used one for three weeks in Southeast Asia with no issues.

Beer and wine are quite expensive relative to everything else—one serving of either will double the price of your meal. A night of partying in Bangkok will cost more than you probably paid for your hotel room. The beer won't win any awards either, but with the weather as hot as it is here, you probably won't care. If you can stomach it, the local rice whisky is much easier on the budget at less than ten bucks for a 750-ml bottle. Lesser-known brands are even cheaper.

Bangkok is a gastronomic delight for those willing to splurge on a fancy restaurant. For the price of an average meal at home, you can eat at some of the best places in town and get a meal you will never forget. Oddly enough, one of the best places to eat well is at the big shopping malls: ones like Central World and Pier 21 have as many restaurants as stores.

At all the beaches, fresh fish and shrimp are abundant and bargain-priced. In Chiang Mai and parts of the northeast, you can sample "jungle cuisine" like python, turtle, and the like. As you may have guessed, vegetarians don't have the easiest time in rural areas. Learn enough Thai to order things without meat in the markets, especially if you don't eat seafood.

Transportation:

Trains and buses are cheap and convenient. An overnight sleeper train bunk from Bangkok to Chiang Mai is around $25 in air-conditioned second-class, less than double that in first-class. A seat to Penang, Malaysia starts at $20 A/C second-class. On the long journeys you can get set meals on board.

Thailand has one of the largest disparities I've ever seen in third to second train seat prices. On the short Bangkok to Ayutthaya ride, we spent a mere 15 baht (50¢) to go one way in third-class, then paid 245 baht ($8) for an air-conditioned second-class seat. Yes, 16 times the price to go from one cabin to the other, for a trip of an hour-and-a-half.

You can travel by train from Bangkok to Singapore in a second-class sleeper for around $65—surely one of the world's best bargains—or first-class for under $200. This is a 48-hour journey in all, so it's best to break it up with some time in Malaysia. (If money is no object, you can do the trip in sumptuous style on the Orient-Express version for $2,200, including drinks and meals.)

Buses are often a cheaper option and go more places, with air-conditioned trips across the country often running less than $20. Shorter hops will run $1 to $2 per hour of travel, less on the ones without A/C. An air-conditioned bus to the Cambodian border is around $7.50.

Local transportation is a bargain in international terms. In Bangkok, river taxis are 50¢, local buses are less than 40¢, and taxis average less than $4 for a half-hour trip. Cabs are metered (starting at $1.15) and drivers are legally required to use them, but you wouldn't know that hanging around the main tourist areas, where flouting this law is common. You have to go through five or six drivers sometimes to find one who will use the meter instead of charging you an inflated flat rate. You can use noisy tuk-tuks for short hauls, but they're bad for your lungs and you'll have to bargain hard. They don't offer much savings over a taxi if you're going more than a short distance.

Elated cries of joy went up when the Bangkok Skytrain and subway finally opened earlier this decade, after years of delays. If either is on your route, they can literally shave hours off a cross-town trip. Prices start at 25¢, with most trips averaging $1-$1.50, and an all-day unlimited pass is $4.50. Neither goes anywhere near Khao San Road, unfortunately.

That is also true for the new train from the Suvarnabhumi Airport, which was finished at the beginning of 2011. It gets you most other places though, since it connects with the Skytrain and Metro. Note that it doesn't run from midnight to 6 am, when many of the international flights seem to arrive. For flying out of Bangkok, it's especially good for Thai Airways since you can check in at the central terminus before riding to the airport.

You can rent a scooter for as little as $5 a day in some areas of the country, although $8 to $12 is more common. Bicycles are generally a buck or three for a few hours to a day.

Many budget airlines have sprung up in Southeast Asia and they have increased competition on many routes, lowering prices. You can fly within the country one-way for less than $50 if you are flexible, and flights to some neighboring countries are cheaper now than they were 10 years ago. Your best bet is to buy these tickets locally in Thailand, if possible, as the options change on a monthly basis.

What Else?
•   Thailand is a great place to get a massage, either in the cities or right on the beach; it's usually $5 to $10 for a whole hour! Even at a spa, the bill is usually less than $20 for an hour with a well-trained masseuse.

- Speaking of pampering, a full facial, manicure, and pedicure in a salon or day spa will run less than $25. (Outside the chain hotels, that is.)
- Admission to museums and attractions is generally $1 to $5 and most Buddhist temples are free, although a donation of a few coins is appreciated.
- A group of you can charter a boat at the beaches for $3 to $10 each—a great way to see the bizarre landscapes around Krabi and the Phi-Phi islands.
- Certified divers can go below for about $40 to $75 a day inclusive (two dives), and snorkeling equipment can be rented for the day for a few dollars. Thailand is on par with Honduras as one of the cheapest places to get an open-water PADI certification course: between $260 and $350 depending on the island.
- It's no secret that drugs are cheap and plentiful, but anyone who takes the risk of indulging should at least do it away from the cities. There are plenty of foreigners locked up in Thai jails who were dumb enough to be caught red-handed, or were set up by the dealer.
- Men can have a suit custom-made in any style, starting at around $90 and generally topping out at $200, including a tailored shirt. Women or men can bring in a photo from a fashion magazine and tailors will copy it in any fabric, including silk. Competition is fierce, so those ordering more than one item can get a whole wardrobe at a big discount.
- Things to buy: silk clothing and ties, woven cotton clothing, wooden and stone statues, jewelry, purses, lacquer-ware, cooking utensils made from coconuts, wall hangings, and bags. For professionals only, it's a good place to buy gems.
- Bangkok's backpacker area is the best place in Southeast Asia to trade in books and to stock up on new ones. Prices are just fair, but the selections are amazing.
- Things you can get for a buck or less: a whole pineapple chopped up for you at a street stall, a kilo of seasonal fruit, a coconut with a straw in it, pad thai at a street stall, a fruit shake, three local bus rides in Bangkok, a four-stop Skytrain

ride, an hour or more at an Internet café, a kilo of your clothes washed and dried.

ASIA

Cambodia

In the first edition I called Cambodia "a poor and bedraggled country that happens to hold Angkor Wat—one of the greatest architectural wonders of the world." If there's one country in this book that has seen the most dramatic turnaround, Cambodia is it. The roads especially have gotten a major makeover. All the main ones you are likely to travel on now are nicely paved. There is a growing infrastructure for tourists on the beaches around Sihanoukville, which wasn't the case just a few years ago. The government has become relatively stable (in a benevolent dictator kind of way) and crime has gone down quite a bit, along with the number of firearms confiscated and voluntarily turned in.

The increased money flow and building boom is a mixed blessing, especially around Angkor Wat. Siem Riep has quickly become a tourist ghetto, with a few luxury hotels vying for space with dozens of chock-a-block concrete buildings thrown up in a hurry, with few regulations. The water table is in serious trouble and some reports indicate that Angkor is actually sinking a bit each year.

Some are grumbling about the progress in Phnom Penh too, which used to come off like a wild-west frontier town, but with French Colonial buildings. (Many of those buildings are getting razed for the sake of "progress.") As a full-page travel article in the *Wall Street Journal* noted recently, "Vendors have stopped selling marijuana in public markets and fun-seekers can no longer lob live grenades behind the military complex outside of town." (You can still fire off an automatic weapon, but at a charge that comes to dollar a bullet.) The brothel crackdown has gotten so bad that the prostitutes gathered together at a temple to pray for relief. Still, when you look on a hotel-booking site online, once you get past the top two or three luxury palaces, the price drops below $120 for the rest, so the city has obviously not hit the big-time yet.

Few countries on earth experienced as much misery and death in the latter half of the 20th century as Cambodia. Still, some travelers fall in love with the place and its people, despite the heartrending tragic history and poverty. There's no denying that Angkor Wat is one of the most spectacular man-made historical structures on the planet, and this alone is reason enough to visit. Few tourists go much beyond this area and the capital, so it's very easy to get away from the crowds and feel like a true explorer. (Just don't go *too* far off the path—land mines are still buried.) For the right kind of traveler, this is a unique experience and you can't beat the prices.

Sadly, most of Cambodia's progress has not trickled down to the masses. Some three-quarters of the population lives in villages without electricity or clean water, and the per capita GDP is a mere $650 per year. Much of the foreign aid that comes in gets siphoned off by corrupt officials instead of going to the people who really need it the most.

Partly as a result of all this, Cambodia vies with Laos as the cheapest place to travel in the region. You can still find decent $1.50 meals and beers for less than a buck during happy hour. A backpacker couple could get by for $20 to $30 a day if staying for a few weeks on a shoestring, sleeping in the cheapest places, and eating where the locals do. Figure $30 to $40 for a shorter trip with more moving around. If eating at better restaurants, and staying at a nicer hotel with hot water and A/C, $50 to $80 a day would allow a big step up in comfort and three daily meals in nicer restaurants with waiters. Angkor Wat is a day's budget by itself, so factor that in and stay a day or two longer.

It's not hard to buy yourself a little comfort for a few more dollars here. An air-conditioned hotel room is easy to find for under $20. You could spend $20-$30 on dinner for two, but it would be a serious splurge in a nice place geared to tourists. With $1.50 beers and $3 main dishes being pretty standard where tourists gather, your money goes a long way even if you're not all that careful with it.

In this chapter when you see prices in dollars, you'll actually pay in dollars. Although Cambodia technically has its own currency, you don't see it in use much outside the local markets. Even the grocery stores list prices in dollars. Good thing too: $20 in the local currency is 80,000 in riels (KHR). That's a lot of zeros to keep track of!

Accommodation:

Cambodia is one of the cheapest places on the planet when it comes to lodging. You can find a hostel bed for as little as $3 and at $5-$6, you'll have a range of them to pick from. Often they'll be in a prime location and have free Wi-Fi. You'll also find plenty of budget backpacker hotels with private rooms between $7 and $20 a night.

Even at the $20 double level, you'll often have hot water, air conditioning, and breakfast included. Spend more than $25 a night and you'll get all that for sure, plus a smiling daily maid. We paid $44 a night for *two* connecting rooms in Siem Reap, including the largest made-to-order breakfast I've ever had in a hotel, for all three of us! It was immaculate and the staff was more attentive than at many big chain hotels in other countries. I saw a brand new hotel near it that had just opened with a sign outside offering rooms for $15 to $35, with breakfast included.

You can often find a triple room for three traveling together or a family. In backpacker places, the prices are usually per person, like $4 single, $8 double, $12 triple. But at more standard hotels, a triple is often not much more than a double—and the single traveler will pay more than half what a couple will.

If you're looking to splurge somewhere without breaking the bank, this can be a good place to do it. Keep in mind that in Siem Reap, most of the high-end hotels are outside the city, where they have more room to sprawl. They can feel kind of isolated if you're there for more than a night or two.

In the capital, a few storied hotels command a premium, but when *Condé Nast Traveler* recently printed a rundown on where to stay, they recommended seven hotels that were $85 or less per night.

The formerly sleepy beach town of Sihanoukville has some of the most expensive hotels in the country now, with a few topping $200 per night. There are plenty right on the water for less than $60, and in town for as little as five bucks. If you follow the backpackers and head further up or down the coast, you'll find more laid-back areas with more simple bungalows to choose from.

Food & Drink:

One night the three of us pored over the menus posted outside a few side-by-side restaurants, looking for one that would make us happy, but that would have something our pickier daughter would eat. We settled on one that looked good and took one of the two remaining tables. We started salivating as we looked at the dishes, helpfully photographed on the laminated menus.

We ordered, we feasted, and we were very satisfied. When the bill came, it was $11 for the following: 3 beers, a coconut shake, spring rolls, noodles with chicken, yellow chicken curry with potatoes, and shrimp curry with coconut. I left a 75¢ tip, which was generous by local standards.

This was a typical dinner bill for us. Only twice did we top $20. My wife's birthday hit while we were in Cambodia, so one night I took her out for a splurge at one of the fanciest places in town. Beautiful food was artfully arranged under designer light fixtures. I blew nearly $50 that night with tip, but for three courses each and a bottle of wine.

There are more than 200 restaurants and 90 bars competing in Siem Reap, more than that in the capital. You won't have much trouble finding a deal.

Cambodian food is at times a bit like Thai, but not as spicy. It's a bit like Vietnamese, but with less fish sauce. It uses a lot of what's local and abundant, including rice, vegetables, lake fish, and coconut. In simple restaurants and market stalls, it can be as little as a dollar a plate. For $2 to $3, you get a waiter and nicer furniture.

Draft beer is often used to get you in the door, so it frequently goes for 50¢ a mug. Oddly enough, one brand is Angkor and the other is Anchor. Don't worry, there's not much difference. Sometimes that low price is just at happy hour, but more than a few restaurants have a withered sign saying "Happy hour 24 hours." The regular price is 70¢ to $2 depending on brand and atmosphere. Cocktails go for $1.50 to $4 each. For whatever reason, imported liquor here is often about the same price as in the U.S. or less, which keeps the prices low. If you choose a local firewater, you can get the proverbial $1 cocktail in some spots.

Fruit shakes are abundant and reasonably priced, often 50¢ to $1.50. Soda and water are less than a dollar in a restaurant. It's best to pack a water purifier, as you'll go through gallons of water in this tropical heat.

Where tourists gather, you can get a good cup of coffee or a latte for $1.50 or so, made with good beans grown in Vietnam.

Transportation:

The transportation situation in Cambodia has gone from abysmal to quite good in the space of a decade. Funds have finally flowed into road repairs and expansions, and it no longer takes a whole day to go 150 kilometers like it did not so long ago. Because of this, investors have felt more confident expanding bus routes and upgrading their fleets.

You can still get from the capital to Siem Reap by boat if you want, but that $35 ticket is no longer the only option. Now the most comfortable air-conditioned bus with W-Fi is $13. Or you can get to Battambang on a less comfortable local one for $4, and to Siem Reap for $6. The local bus from Phnom Penh to the beaches runs $4 to $6.

When it comes to border crossings, it's the old trade-off between time/money and comfort/money. In theory, you can take a bus between the capital and Ho Chi Minh City in Vietnam for as little as $6. But most people are glad they spent the $12-14 for a better and quicker bus or boat/bus combo. Or if you want to skip the south or are on a vacation timeline, you can fly. We got tickets to Danang for $160 each last-minute.

Getting from Bangkok to Siem Reap (or vice-versa) is still an ordeal, but it now can easily be done in one day and on better roads. It's a two-part process: you pay to get to the border, cross it, and then need to pay again to get the rest of the way. The bus from the Cambodian border town to Siem Reap is $9, a taxi $48 for up to four people. Between there and Bangkok you take a bus or train.

Taxi or tuk-tuk rides in Cambodia are dirt-cheap. We had a tuk-tuk driver for the whole day at Angkor Wat for $14. He waited for us each time and took off to the next spot when we were ready. Rides around town in the capital or Siem Reap are $1-$3. (When there's a meter, it starts at $1 for 2 kilometers.) You can hire one to take you hours away—such as Sihanoukville to Phnom Penh—for around $50 to $60. Or hire a car and driver for the day to tour around for $25 to $35.

The cheapest option for getting around is on a motorcycle taxi. You hop on the back and get to where you need to go for a dollar or so. (Obviously this works better when you don't have your backpack!) If you hire a *motodup* to get around the temples of Angkor, you'll pay a shade more than half what a tuk-tuk costs: $6-9 instead of $12-$16. So unless you're traveling alone, the latter is a better deal - and you have sun protection.

You're not allowed to rent your own motorbike in Siem Reap, but you can in other places for as little as $6 a day for a scooter, $15 to $25 per day for a real motorcycle. Weekly deals are widely available for $100 or so.

Bike rentals are $1 to $3 a day and you can tour a fair number of the main Angkor ruins by bike from Siem Reap.

What Else?

• At the time this book went to press, entrance to Angkor Wat was $20 for one day, $40 for three days (they do not need to be consecutive), or $60 for a week. Compared to sites like Petra or even Machu Picchu, this is a terrific bargain, especially if you stick around a while and go back. There's really way too much to see in one day anyway.

• This may be the cheapest country in the world in which to get a massage. It's easy to find a one-hour massage for $6 or less, and some offer a four-hand massage (two people working out your kinks) for $10. Spa treatments like exfoliation, manicures, and pedicures start at $3.

• Tours booked locally are a good way to get out of the main cities and see the local countryside. Figure on $15 to $35 per person for an all-day tour depending on meals, distance, and whether equipment such as bikes or boats are involved. Adventure tours on horseback, mountain bike, dirt bike, or ATV are on offer by agencies in the main tourist centers. Or play paintball for $6.

• Don't ask me why, but there are eight mobile phone carriers fighting it out in this small country, so you can get a SIM card for as little as $5 and make phone calls home for under 10¢ a minute.

• As in Thailand, there's a relatively liberal attitude toward gay and lesbian travelers, and in the capital there are usually four or five regular clubs and a few rotating nights catering to that crowd at others.

• What to buy: silk handicrafts and clothing, bags made from rice sacks, scarves, wood carvings, pirated music and movies, and lacquer products.

• What you can get for a buck or less: a street stall meal, 3 croissants or baguettes, a haircut, a half-pound of peeled garlic, two pounds of rice, an ice cream cone, a pound of shallots, two papayas, an hour or two of Internet café access, a short tuk-tuk ride or longer motorbike taxi ride, two happy hour beers, a local liquor cocktail, a fruit shake, two packs of mosquito coils, a full MP3 album put on your iPod/iPhone.

ASIA

Indonesia

Thick guidebooks with microscopic type have been written on Indonesia, but the authors still have to apologize about areas that they've barely covered. The world's fourth most-populous nation is composed of thousands of islands, many of which are as different as day and night. With people on them that have almost nothing in common with those islands three ferry stops away. Most visitors stop in Bali, Java, or Sumatra (in that order of popularity), but exotic locales such as Lombok, Komodo, Sulawesi, Flores, and old Borneo offer plenty more to see and do.

Each island is host to a unique culture and it's hard to generalize about common aspects. Sumatra has some of the cheapest prices amidst amazing, unspoiled scenery, and travel there gets easier each year. Java can boast great artists, musicians, and dancers, and is home to stupendous monuments and active volcanoes.

Bali is either getting to or is past the point of being able to sustain the number of visitors it receives, which has gone from 1.2 million in 2001 to 2.5 million in 2011. That's around 40% of the whole country's total. Most of those visitors are in the south, where traffic has gotten horrendous and pollution is a serious problem. Other parts of the island are still like an aesthetic picture postcard, with a unique culture that refuses to fade away.

Sulawesi offers the strange Torajan culture and architecture inland, as well as some of the best diving and snorkeling around on the coasts. There are also kickback island beaches, surfing spots, the Komodo dragon, a volcano crater with lakes of different colors, and a great variety of village architecture and customs as you go island hopping.

Unfortunately, none of this comes without some risk. The world's biggest Muslim country by population has had plenty of violent flare-ups over the years, both aimed at outsiders and aimed at each other (mostly Muslims vs. Christians). Or in Aceh's case, aimed at the government and anyone seen as not conservative enough: the local government closed 16 Christian churches in 2012 and arrested 65 people at a Banda Aceh punk club, shaving kids' Mohawks and removing their piercings. In general, the national government has done a good job of ensuring security in the past decade, but some say they've let too many fundamentalist bullies slide in local scuffles. Do your homework and check up on the current political situation. Compare the problem areas to a map; this is a very large country.

The visa situation in Indonesia has changed several times over the past decade and has swung back to a more reasonable place lately. Most nationalities can now get a visa on arrival for 30 days and—here's the key part—you can now renew it for another 30 days without leaving the country. If you live in a consular area like New York or London, you can apply for a 60-day one in advance.

The Indonesian people themselves are overwhelmingly warm and friendly, and the language is one of the easiest to learn on the planet. Shopping is a blast if you don't mind patient bargaining. This is a place where you'll be quoted a price three times what the item actually goes for in the end, and you need four local digits in rupiah for the equivalent of one dollar, so carry a calculator.

Prices fluctuate with currency changes, the state of fuel subsidies, and rice prices, but in relative terms this is often the cheapest destination on the planet when comparing places that actually have a decent infrastructure. With the Indonesian rupiah continually coming under pressure, and supply still outweighing demand for hotel rooms and tours outside of Bali, there is no real chance of runaway price inflation like we've seen in Eastern Europe and Turkey. Companies complained in late 2012 when the minimum wage went up to $228 per *month.*

Two people together can travel on $25 to $40 per day fairly easily in Sumatra, northern Bali, and parts of Java, and generally under $50 elsewhere except on Borneo. (For a single traveler, as little as $15 per day on the standard backpacker routes.) In most parts of the country, $40 to $70 per day allows a couple to live in comfortable flash packer territory, and spending more than $100 a day would mean staying in nice hotels with a pool, hiring taxis and drivers a lot, and eating and drinking to your heart's content almost anywhere in town. Anyone with hard currency will find an infinite list of bargains here.

If you do want to splurge, you can on Bali especially, but you don't have to make a lot of sacrifices if you're not in that lofty range—paying what a local person makes in six months for one night's lodging. When people go over budget here, it's usually because of having to take a few flights to cover long distances, not because of costs on the ground.

Be advised that the economy is growing rapidly here, at a pace of 6.5% a year, and the ranks of the middle class (defined here as earning more than $3,000 per year) should pass the majority level in a year or so after this book hits the shelves. The number of millionaires is on pace to double within a few years. That means more traffic in already hopelessly gridlocked Jakarta (car sales are rising 10% year-over-year), more motorbikes on the roads (8 million sold in 2011), and more domestic competition for those guesthouse rooms and bus seats. Don't wait too long to take advantage of what has traditionally been one of the best values on the planet for travelers.

Accommodation:

For guesthouse prices, there's now Bali and "not Bali." Ubud used to be one of the world's greatest lodging deals, but then the glossy magazines started hyping it, *Eat Pray Love* came out, and that was that. Even there you can find a very basic room for $6 or so, but figure $12 and up for something you'll actually like. Add more for hot water and A/C.

On the other thousands of islands, you can still occasionally find a rural budget *losmen* (guesthouse) for around $3 double per night for a basic room with a shared bath. Finding one for $6 or less is not very difficult anywhere outside the big cities. Showers are often nonexistent at this level; you use a *mandi* to dump buckets of water over yourself. Spend just a couple dollars more than the bottom level, however, and the value is outstanding. In parts of Sulawesi and Sumatra, you can rent a huge room with a private bath and verandah, surrounded by lush tropical gardens, for $7 or so, including breakfast.

There aren't a lot of hostels, but often you can negotiate a better price on a double room in a half-empty hotel if it's just one person. There are plenty of triples around for threesomes and families.

For $8 to $15 you'll often get a huge fan-cooled room with a king-sized bed, towels, maid service, and breakfast. In some spots, for as little as $15 double you can get an air-conditioned room with room service and a swimming pool outside your door. On Samosir Island in Lake Toba, a family can rent a two-bedroom suite on the lake for just a tad more.

At the top end of the scale, it's possible to spend $300 in Jakarta or several times that at one of Bali or Lombok's lavish resorts, but it's normally quite difficult to spend over $100 elsewhere in the country; $40 to $80 will usually cover a 4-star-equivalent room if it's not high season or a holiday.

Food & Drink:

Indonesian food varies by region (especially in terms of spiciness), but is usually some variation of noodle or rice dishes, with interesting ingredients such as jackfruit, peanut sauce, and coconut thrown in, resulting in interesting taste sensations. You can nearly always get what would be called "free range chicken" in the western world; here it's a scrawny bird that's been running around the back lot. You'll find loads of bargain-priced fish on the coasts (and there are a lot of coasts). Snacks and sweets are excellent in the markets.

Meals can be as little as 50¢ each on the street, a buck or two in most simple restaurants. Touristy restaurants in Bali can cost many times that, but even there you'd be hard pressed to spend over $15 on a three-course meal with drinks if you avoid the five-star hangouts. In most non-urban parts of the country, $15 for two is a real splurge.

In some spots, you sit down at a table where a waiter sets a dozen or more plates in front of you. You sample whatever you want, and at the end the waiter counts up what's been eaten and gives you a bill. The tab is usually far lower than what you'd expect (especially if you just arrived) and you walk out stuffed.

Cleanliness levels vary quite a bit though. It's often safest to eat in backpacker hangouts, busy locals' joints, or at clean-looking street stalls where you can see everything being prepared. Be skeptical about meat, although seafood is generally okay if it's fresh—and in a nation of islands it usually is. Avoid the tap water at all costs; carry a purifier, drink tea, or drink bottled/filtered water.

Beer prices have continued to creep up across Indonesia. A small Bintang, Bali Hai, or San Miguel averages $1.50 in a bar, but you'll more often see the larger bottles at $2.50 and up. If 75% didn't go to taxes, it would be even cheaper. The coffee is absolutely heavenly. A few cups of this java (at 35¢ or so if it's not a fancy cafe) and you'll wonder why anyone could possibly drink instant coffee here.

Transportation:
This is not Thailand or Malaysia—getting from point A to point B is usually cheap, but seldom comfortable if you're

taking the least expensive option. A backbreaking economy train seat from Jakarta to Yogyakarta is only about $15, but for less than $40 you can go first-class with the local businessmen, with A/C, reclining seats, and meal service. Buses are more comfortable on Java ($8 to $40 for long hauls), but are often crowded and bumpy on the other islands.

On the smaller islands, travel is by *bemo*—a converted mini-van built to seat tiny local butts and legs. It's not unusual to see a small Toyota van stuffed with 20 people! For this privilege you'll be charged two or three times what the locals pay unless you bargain diligently. On Bali and on some popular traveler routes, however, you can buy a less cramped seat on tourist shuttles (for a much higher price of course).

Indonesia long had some of the cheapest bus and ferry transport prices in the world because of fuel subsidies, but the government couldn't keep sustaining those and prices have crept up. Even when gas was cheap they stuffed every bus and minivan to the gills, so pad your budget a bit assuming you'll get worn out dealing with this and need to upgrade sometimes—especially if you're tall—or will decide to fly.

Domestic flight prices are all over the map here and unfortunately, so are the reputations of the airlines flying those routes. Indonesian airlines were banned from flying into the EU because of their safety record, but that ban was lifted on four of them in 2009, and this has become one of the most competitive air travel markets in Asia. Check with a local agency or dig around online to see the options. It's hard to keep up with who flies where and what current fares are like.

To go between the small islands, modern ferries can be under $10, though the overnight ones require a cabin charge to avoid sleeping on the deck or crowded hold below. Chartering a boat for a few days to island-hop on the open seas is another option: generally $15 to $25 per day per person for a basic journey depending on the trip and what the meals are like. For a real cabin rather than a mattress on the deck for Flores to Lombok (4 nights), figure on $35 to $60 per day, but with full board that's not very hard on the budget.

Motorcycle or scooter rentals are $3 to $8 a day depending on location and condition; bicycles are usually a dollar or two per day. Gasoline is still subsidized and as this book went to press was set to rise to 6,000 rupiah (less than 75¢) per liter.

Local car taxis are hard to find in many towns; most residents travel by bemo or tricycle rickshaws known as *becaks*. It's fairly easy, however, to find a private driver for trips between cities, for the price of cab ride at home. Hiring a driver usually makes more sense than renting a car financially and is less hassle.

What Else?

•   Indonesia boasts the largest diversity of marine life in the world. Naturally the snorkeling is fantastic in numerous locations, with equipment rentals averaging $2 to $4 per day. Scuba trips are widely available for $20 to $35 a dive.

•   Indonesia is reportedly home to 17% of the world's bird species and the world's largest lizard—the Komodo dragon—lives on Komodo Island. (The lizards have attacked and killed a few villagers now and then, so treat them with the proper fear and respect.)

•   You can take a one or two-day batik course in Yogyakarta or Solo for as little as $6 per day, plus a few dollars more for your self-designed T-shirt or sarong.

•   Admission to the country's best-known monuments on Java has nearly doubled since 2008. The local administrator in charge told the Jakarta Post, "The increase is necessary to raise money for promotional purposes among other things, and to target tourists from Australia and South Korea." So in other words, you'll now pay $20 to enter Borobudur or $13 to enter Prambanan so they can spend more on advertising in Korea. Nice. By the way, the locals pay $3 to enter. Thankfully the average elsewhere in the country is a fraction of this and some museum admissions are just 2000 rupiah—25¢ or so, depending on the rate.

•   Impressive dance performances, accompanied by full gamelan orchestra, range from $3 to $6 in places where backpackers congregate, and often include transportation to the site. Shadow puppet shows are cheap, but get boring quickly if you don't understand the language. On Sumatra, there's a whole different kind of music and dance, which is simpler and more upbeat.

• Volcano hikes are a grueling, but an unforgettable experience for the adventurous. If you arrange it locally, expect to pay $7 to $20 for the whole package: a guide, transportation, and a meal or two. You can usually rent camping equipment for 2-day trips. The sunrise scenery, with the volcanoes poking through the clouds, is an image that you won't soon forget.

• Things to buy: woodcarvings, batik paintings and clothing, shadow puppets, silver jewelry, bead jewelry, and numerous local crafts. Ubud (in Bali), Yogyakarta (in Java) and Lake Toba (in Sumatra) offer the widest selection of goods. You can also find some interesting crafts in the Toraja area of Sulawesi. Outside of the areas where luxury travelers pay high list prices without knowing any better, driving a hard bargain is a bit sadistic. You can literally be arguing over pennies and that difference could be dinner for the vendor's family. The first price quoted is usually laughably high, so bargain well, but with a smile.

• What you can get for a buck or less: two noodle dishes or soups at a simple stall, a shirt, two hours of rowboat rental, bike rental for a half-day, a visit to a couple of attractions or museums, a haircut and shave, a two-hour bus ride, a short taxi ride, two or three huge papayas. And food for thought: a dollar or two pays for a month of school for a rural family's child.

ASIA

Malaysia

Malaysia was already more expensive than Thailand or Vietnam when I first passed through the region two decades ago, and it has continued to develop (and get more expensive) since then. It's still in this book because overall it's still a good value. Prices aren't rock-bottom for any aspect of travel, but food, lodging, and transportation all seem reasonable for what you get—and can be lower than some resort areas in Thailand. It's still less expensive than comparable destinations on other continents.

Peninsular Malaysia is more westernized than Thailand or Indonesia, so it's a good first stop for those not quite ready to give up the comforts of home, o r a good way to sample the exotic while still being relatively sure you'll have a clean place to eat and a western toilet in your room. Transportation is easy and comfortable, a lot of people speak English, and you can even drink the water in most locations. There are seldom any clashes between the various ethnic groups and religions. On the other hand, some consider it "spoiled," free speech is only occasionally tolerated, and it'll bust your budget in a hurry to do much partying here—when you can find a drink.

The main attractions on the peninsula are the jungle interior and the beautiful beaches. The cities are generally not worth an extended stay, especially Kuala Lumpur. Georgetown (on Penang) has a nice atmosphere, with lots of interesting

Chinese temples, and is well set up for travelers in transit. The Cameroon Highlands make for a pleasant retreat from the heat, and the old Portuguese port of Malacca provides an interesting mixed bag of colonial and Chinese architecture.

Visitors generally don't tend to spend weeks on end in Malaysia, unless they find one of those picture-perfect tropical islands that they can't bear to leave. (With Malaysia claiming some 20,000 islands, it happens.) Most nationalities get 30 or 60 days to visit upon arrival, no advance visa required.

Adventurous types head to Sabah or Sarawak on the island of Borneo, which are a whole different world—some say more of a "true" Malaysia since the population is almost entirely ethnic Malays. Prices and comforts are quite erratic in this part of the country, though and it's no secret that the jungle is disappearing at an alarming rate. Malaysia is not known for having a strong environmental stance.

A single traveler can get by on $25 to $40 per day on the peninsula if not moving around too much. Couples should budget $45 to $75. Mid-range travelers should multiply that figure two or three times. A typical beach tab for a bamboo bungalow, meals, and snorkeling equipment can be as low as $35 a day for a couple on some of the islands.

Malaysia is a big medical tourism destination, with prices that can be 1/10 of what it costs in the U.S. for the same procedure. Local expats talk about $8 doctor visits, dental cleanings/x-rays for $30, and Lasik surgery from the best doctor in the country for less than $500.

If you are looking for a tropical retirement paradise, Malaysia is one of the few Asian countries actively trying to lure more foreigners. If you meet certain requirements on assets and pension income for the "My Second Home" program, there are plenty of incentives on offer. You can buy property outright here just like a local, with no restrictions.

Accommodation:
A beach bungalow or guesthouse room usually starts at about $8 for something very basic, although you can

sometimes find a dorm bed for $5. The cities are much more expensive—you can easily pay $25 for a grotty room in Kuala Lumpur. Most of these are typical Chinese-owned hotels: simple places that cover the basics, with few frills or services. If you can up your budget to $50 to $75, on the other hand, you'll have a nice chain-type hotel room, all the trimmings included.

Outside the cities, you'll pay $5 to $12 for a dorm bed, $8 to $16 for a basic room with a private bath, and a mid-range hotel with TV and A/C starts at about $18, with $24 to $40 being the norm. There's usually a lot to choose from in that range so you can be pickier, but even at the $10 to $20 range you'll have a variety of options in places like Penang and Malacca.

The sky's the limit at the very top end, especially in the capital and resort areas, but in most of the country it is usually no sweat to find something quite nice for $50 to $75. That would be a chain-type hotel with elevator, pool, restaurants, room service, and a bellhop.

Food & Drink:
Meals are seldom dull in Malaysia because you usually have three cuisines to choose from: Malay, Chinese, and Indian. The latter two are cooked by descendants of Chinese and Indian nationals who were brought in by the British when the country was still a colony. Street stall or food market meals are $1 to $3 with sodas, even in the cities. Local or backpacker sit-down restaurants are only a little bit more. You can go from stall to stall in Penang and have a world-class feast.

Even the top-end restaurants are quite reasonable by western standards. Usually $10 to $20 will cover a three-course meal in a fine restaurant—until you order alcohol.

This is a good country in which to let your liver recover. Beer is expensive for the region: generally $3 and up for a 12-oz. bottle due to high taxes. You can pay more than you would at home in a nice place. Local commercial whiskey is a cheaper option, starting at $5 per bottle, but is scary. *Arak* (a local rice whiskey) is even less money if you can stomach it. Carrying or selling drugs can result in the death penalty, but that doesn't mean the country is low on junkies.

There's plenty of fresh, tropical fruit juice for cheap wherever you go, and you can safely drink the water in most of the towns and cities. Coffee is usually a letdown, but the situation is getting better each year in the cities.

Transportation:

The train line in Malaysia is not too convenient—it only runs through the interior—but it's good for getting to Thailand from Kota Bahru (on the east side) or Georgetown/Penang (on the west). Prices start at about $15 for a cross-country trip or $18 for an excursion to Bangkok, just a few dollars for a short haul.

Malaysia has some of the best roads in the world, so buses are faster and more convenient, plus often they are the only option. All are air-conditioned to the point of being traveling meat lockers and they travel at speeds you don't really want to know about—sit away from the front or close your eyes! Tickets run from a few dollars to more than $20 for a long trip. A ride from Kuala Lumpur to Georgetown is a bargain $10 for a first-class bus, from KL to Malacca just $4. A bus from there to Singapore is less than $30. Almost all of the upper-end ones offer free Wi-Fi.

Big Mercedes share-taxis are a quick way to go between towns. After bargaining, a 100-km trip will cost $5-$10 each.

Local buses are comfortable and reasonably priced in the cities: they start at 35¢ and max out at $1 for a four-zone trip across the capital. Taxis are easy to flag down or call for in the cities, rickshaws exist in some of the smaller towns, and bicycle rickshaws are still around in Sabah and Sarawak. Taxis are reasonable overall at and official rate of around $3 for 5 kilometers, although it's 50% more at night. You can get to most parts of KL from the international airport by taxi for $15 or less in a regular cab (or for as little as $3 on public transportation).

What Else?

• Museums and attractions are a bargain: the small but excellent National Museum in KL is only 60¢.

• Snorkeling and diving are quite good off the islands. Expect to pay $2 to $5 to rent snorkeling equipment for the day, $25 to $45 per dive for scuba.

• Shopping is just fair in peninsular Malaysia—save your souvenir dollars for other places unless you're going to Sabah or Sarawak. You'll also need to get your news elsewhere: press freedom is getting closer, but there's serious censorship.

• Cell phone service is widespread and cheap here. Buy a local SIM card for your unlocked phone for a few dollars.

• What you can get for a buck or less: some Chinese food on the street, lots of snacks, a large glass of fresh star fruit or guava juice, admission to many museums, popcorn at your $4 movie, two city bus rides, three local newspapers (that all say the same thing), a half-hour of Internet access, a few pounds of mangoes.

ASIA

Laos

I once wrote: "Laos is one of those rare destinations where travelers can still feel like they've beaten the pack." Alas, all good things must come to an end and now this former backwater is a full-blown backpacker magnet.

Vientiane is still one of the sleepiest capital cities around, but it is growing fast and more motorbikes hit the nice, new roads each week. This is the only real city, with Luang Prabang being the main tourist stop, and Vang Vieng being the must-visit backpacker town for boozing it up at riverside bars and floating down the river on inner tubes. After at least 27 people died in 2011 doing that and other not so bright acts (like swinging on rope swings into rocky waters when the water was low), the government cracked down and shut a whole slew of bars. Time will tell if we hit a happy medium between the way it was (when tourists were rare) and the way it got (travelers outnumbering locals 15 to 1 and having no sensibility about local norms or culture).

In general, still-communist Laos has been content to sit quietly in the corner, forsaking the mad rush for tourism and investment dollars pursued by Thailand and Vietnam. Tourism still seems like kind of a hobby here: the official Laos Tourism website looks like it was put together by a high school student. They're not buying glossy ads in magazines or bringing loads of writers over on press junkets. Most of the marketing has been word of mouth.

If you get off the well-worn trail, most of this sparsely populated nation is still wild and undeveloped, with rustic bamboo villages dotting nearly all of the countryside. Sometimes too wild: this is not a place where you want to ride a motorbike alone, looking wealthy, in the middle of nowhere.

The country is picking up the pace on its own terms, however, especially in terms of facilities for visitors. In the 1990s you couldn't find a hotel in the whole country that charged more than $100 per night. Now the jet set is spending ungodly sums for the best properties in Vientiane and Luang Prabang. Vang Vieng has become a pure backpacker ghetto and has little of Laos left in it, but you've got to admit, they showed they could build to meet demand.

Otherwise, commercialism is still pretty rare. Apart from loudspeakers blasting communist anthems in the morning in some towns, you're not assaulted by much of anything. Few billboards or in-your-face advertisements for anything are around, and there are even fewer touts or scams to avoid.

The countryside scenes are like something straight out of an old explorer's drawing and some areas outside of Vang Vieng are reminiscent of old Chinese paintings, pointy peaks and all. Perhaps best of all, you can observe a country where tourism has not had a huge impact, where everyone hasn't learned to view you as a walking dollar sign—yet. You need to bargain regularly to avoid getting ripped off: communist countries tend to instill a sense that it's okay to soak the foreigners whenever possible.

There are no huge monuments or "must see" attractions, but the whole city of Luang Prabang is a UNESCO World Heritage site. It's a small, pleasant city made for walking and biking, filled with beautiful Buddhist temples and monks galore. There are some interesting side trips from here as well.

The capital city of Vientiane also has its share of temples and a bizarre Buddha sculpture park that's definitely worth experiencing.

Two people can tour the country for $20 to $40 per day as budget travelers, much less in the villages, where both standards and costs take a dive. This is a country where a single traveler can still get by for less than $15 a day if being really frugal.

The excellent food is a serious willpower test, however, so a little more money will make life more pleasant—and your sleep after dinner less sweaty at night. Outside the three main tourist areas and maybe Pakse, it would be hard for a mid-range couple to spend much over $60 to $80 a day unless going on a lot of adventure tours. Spending $100 per person per day would only be possible if staying at the fanciest hotels, eating at the most expensive restaurant, and ordering imported French wine with lunch and dinner. If you book yourself on a tour that costs $350 a day per person (as I've seen advertised), be assured that at least half that money is going to the tour agency.

The Lao currency, the kip, has gotten more stable the past few years, but the Thai baht is considered a hard currency here. At around 8,800 kip to the U.S. dollar as this book was being put together, you might want to carry around a calculator and wear P^cubed pants with big pockets. The largest bank note is barely worth $10 and you'll have trouble finding change for it. You need to bring ample cash as well, or spend some time hanging out at banks: as hard as it may be to believe this day and age, there are only a handful of ATM facilities in the main cities and the daily limit is restricted to around $70. The machines frequently run out of cash. You can use U.S. dollars for many purchases and banks themselves can distribute higher sums inside.

Accommodation:

Throughout Laos, it pays to travel with a partner; there are not all that many single rooms, and dorms are almost nonexistent. For a double room, the capital is much more expensive than the rest of the country. While $8 will get you a dingy hotel with troubled plumbing in Vientiane, it will get you a lovely hotel room with a four-poster bed in other towns.

Basic guesthouses start at around $4 for a double with shared bath. There are plenty of places under $7 that will provide a private bath with hot water and maybe even throw in maid service and towels. For $10 and up you'll start getting air conditioning and other nice additions. In the dirt road villages, however, facilities are limited. You might only pay a dollar or two a person, but your guesthouse will charitably be described as "spartan." All over the country choices are opening up all the time. While any old hovel with spare rooms could get business before in Vientiane, now they actually have to clean the place.

At the middle and high ranges, Laos is one of the world's great bargains. For the price of a budget motel at home, you'll get something special. Many mid-range properties are atmospheric French Colonial mansions or former royal residences, loaded with amenities for $25-$75 per night. Shelling out $10 more than the standard rate will often put you into a suite.

If you're paying the equivalent rate of a 4-star airport hotel at home, you should be in a palatial room, in an elegant hotel, and have people waiting on you hand and foot.

Food & Drink:

It's not famous, but the food in Laos is often fantastic. It has been influenced by Chinese, Thai, French, and Vietnamese cuisine, so there are always some interesting combinations of meat, rice, vegetables, and noodles. Even the street food is fresh and delicious—usually some kind of noodle soup, often for a dollar or so. You can always find crusty baguettes.

A great meal in a simple restaurant will often come in under $5 for two people. In Vientiane, you can find similar cheap meals, but you'll probably be tempted to go up a notch at least once. Here you can get a full-fledged French dinner for two for under $20, including drinks. The scores of foreign aid workers have definitely upped the level of refinement, and there are plenty of choices where you can easily spend the equivalent of a local worker's monthly salary if you want.

You can also find some great bakeries, which is a rarity in this part of the world. For the road-weary traveler, a cup of good coffee and a pastry in the morning can do wonders, especially when your bill is less than two bucks.

The national beer, Beerlao, is thankfully more interesting than its name. It's usually around $1.50 for a 20-ounce bottle and can sometimes be found on draft for a buck. Imports are rare and double the price, except for the odd Chinese beer brought down the river.

Lao Lao is homemade rice liquor that could probably double as motorcycle fuel in a pinch. It's ridiculously cheap at around $1.50 a liter—cheaper than bottled water sometimes— and goes into all kinds of punches and mixed drinks at backpacker bars.

Service has traditionally been laughably bad in restaurants, especially outside the capital, but it's getting better as a younger generation grows up being around lots more tourists. If you're in a hurry, eat at a street stall. Otherwise, settle in for a leisurely meal, even if you're the only customer in the place.

Transportation:

Transportation costs have gone up with the price of fuel rising, so keep that in mind if looking at old guidebooks or articles.

Travel is primarily by speedboat or barge on the Mekong River, by rickety airplane, or on buses that range from express VIP air-conditioned buses to seats on the back of a pickup truck. None of the options are known for being too comfortable, but the scenery and insight into local culture usually make up for it.

Barely over half of the country's roads are paved, but the main ones get better each year. The mountain road between Luang Prabang and the capital is now relatively smooth sailing. Several buses make this trip each day and if you can spare a few more dollars, it's worth it. Figure on around $1 per hour of travel for the worst bus and about $2 an hour for the very best VIP one, if it's available. Minivans offer door-to-door service from traveler hotels for a bit more money.

On less traveled routes, however (including the hill tribe areas in the north), expect to bounce around on the back of a converted pick-up truck for hours, breathing in lots of dust. Ironically, prices go up according to time in transit and the scarcity of travelers; the worse the ride, the more it will probably cost you for remote areas.

The two-day slow Mekong barge trip from Huay Xai to Luang Prabang ($15 to $30) isn't all that comfortable, but it's a highlight for many visitors. A noisy speedboat can do the trip in a day for double the price. As roads get a bit better and buses offer cheaper rides, these boats are becoming more of a tourist trip than a local one. You'll need to find other backwater routes to really feel like an explorer. In general the other long ones are $12 to $15.

Local flights are quite reasonable, usually $40 to $100 one-way. Popular routes fill up fast, so booking ahead is essential.

City buses in the capital cost only 20¢. Bike rentals everywhere average $1 to $4 per day. (Many of the Chinese bikes have "Highly Dependable" embossed on the frame, but don't bet on it.) Motorcycle rentals are $4 to $10 where they are allowed. Bargain for tuk-tuk style taxis, which are generally $1.50 to $3 to get where you need to go. Hiring a car and driver is generally far cheaper than renting a car yourself: commonly $20 to $35 a day, depending on your bargaining skills and the current price of fuel.

You can fly into the capital or arrive at the Thailand/Laos border by bus or train in several places. Crossing from Vietnam is much more expensive, but is another option.

What Else?
•   In Luang Prabang you can get a massage and a sauna visit for about $5 and hour-long massages for $5 are easy to find.

• Marijuana grows wild all over the country and sells for less than $3 an ounce. (It's often sold by old ladies in the market, who also change money—one stop shopping!) It can show up in shakes and pizzas sometimes, along with magic mushrooms. The police don't seem to be too bothered about it, but technically the penalties can be harsh. Opium has been dealt with more seriously by the government, but is still a staple of blank-staring men in small villages.

• Things to buy: t-shirts with nonsense English on them, baskets, woven and embroidered clothing, and Buddhist amulets.

• If you'd like to stick around for a while, you can rent a house in the capital for under $200 per month, even less further afield.

• What you can get for a buck or less: a noodle soup lunch or two at a street stall, two cups of coffee, three servings of six-chili papaya salad (som tam), two gigantic pineapples chopped up, two bunches of bananas, a large fruit shake or two, bike rental for half a day, a short tuk-tuk ride, a bottle of lao-lao, a haircut and a shave, a kilo of laundry washed and dried, admission to almost anything.

ASIA

Vietnam

Vietnam conjures up plenty of images in American minds, with a vacation spot often not being the first thing that comes up. The country's popularity keeps increasing rapidly, however, to the point where Halong Bay alone gets more than a million foreign tourists a year. The "American War" is all but forgotten (except in deifying Ho Chi Minh) and this former communist rip-off center is now welcoming the world's capitalists with wide-open arms.

Vietnam remains one of the fastest-growing tourism markets in the world, with more than six million visitors, and the pace of development feels a bit *too* frenetic, especially in the two largest cities. This destination remains one of the world's best travel values and if you go soon you'll see it before the big building boom goes from "robust" to "completely out of control." (When it comes to traffic in Saigon and pollution controls in all the cities, we may already be there.)

In many ways, this country of 89 million people—more than Germany—is another one vying for the "most improved" title compared to when the first edition of *The World's Cheapest Destinations* came out. The two-tiered pricing system is gone, meaning some attractions are cheaper now than they were 10 years ago. Younger, more business-savvy entrepreneurs have discovered the rewards of running an honest business at fair prices, beating out the shady competitors through better online reviews.

You'll still be overcharged a lot, especially in the north: the communist "soak the tourists" mentality is still pervasive with street vendors, although it's far less blatant now than it was when I first visited in the 1990s. The vendors have gotten less pushy and the government no longer charges foreigners two or three times what the locals pay for transportation. You'll still feel like a walking stack of money sometimes, with everyone you encounter trying to get a piece, but if you've come overland from Cambodia, you'll feel less pressure from vendors and touts at least. As the country's economy keeps cranking and the population gets richer, there's not as much desperation in the air.

Two could scrape by on as little as $30 per day here staying rather stationary in the countryside, but $40 to $50 per day is more realistic for a couple of budget backpackers, more if you're doing something silly like trying to cover the length of the country in one week.

In the middle range, a couple could do pretty well on $50 to $100 per day, with quite nice lodging, though there is not always a lot of "middle" to be found when it comes to transportation. The luxury and group convention areas are where the government is putting most of its development money, focusing on expensive city hotels and sprawling beach resorts.

The strategy is only halfway working so far: there's a lot of competition for those guests in this part of the world, so prices remain competitive once you get past the top two or three prestige hotels in a given city. My family of three had no problem sticking to a $150 per day budget for everything in 2012, even counting the best possible overnight train tickets from Hue to Hanoi, staying in nice triple rooms with A/C and private bath with fluffy towels, and eating at a lot of good restaurants. So for $200 a day the average couple could really live it up in style.

With a coastline as long as the US west coast, there are plenty of beaches to choose from. Beautiful Ha Long Bay leaves even the most jaded travelers breathless. You'll also find soaring mountains, waterfalls, jungles, and hill-tribe treks that aren't as commercialized as Thailand's. Most of the beauty here is of the natural type: the older architecture was wooden and most has long since vanished, outside Hué anyway. To see much of the older stone Chan temples, you'll have to visit the museum in Da Nang.

Many educated locals speak English in Vietnam, especially in the south. The language is tonal (like Chinese or Thai), but the writing uses Roman letters with accent marks.

It is hard to tour some areas on your own: everything is geared toward groups. You'll actually spend more money trying to do things like hopping around Halong Bay or touring the Mekong Delta independently. Give up and go with the flow. The tours are generally inexpensive and well run if you ask around and find out who is good. Fortunately, there are more of these to choose from all the time. When I visited in the late 1990s, I couldn't find a kayaking trip or rental place on Halong Bay despite days of effort. Now there are a whole slew of operators to pick from there and elsewhere.

Sightseeing can be expensive in some areas and other spots are way overrated when compared to comparable sights in nearby countries. At the same time, many terrific museums are just a dollar or two, a fraction of that for kids.

Avoid the 3-week Tet holiday period in late January/early February; it's a madhouse and rooms are hard to find at any price. There's also a summer family vacation period that sucks up a lot of rooms in popular vacation areas.

Also, get your Facebook fix before you arrive here or you'll be frustrated. It's officially not available in communist Vietnam, so hotels have to use a proxy server or some other workaround for you to get on. Many coffee shops and Internet cafes don't bother.

Also get a guidebook or good app to be aware of scams, annoyances, and what to avoid. Start with guidance on how to cross the street properly amidst an onslaught of motorbike traffic that must be seen to be believed.

Despite the madness you'll encounter on the streets and barely passable sidewalks, there's a lot to uncover in Vietnam, the food is interesting, and one study found the locals to be the second-happiest people in the world behind Costa Rica.

Accommodation:

Guesthouse prices in Vietnam aren't as cheap at the bottom end as in neighboring countries, but the quality is uniformly high in the main destinations. Western toilets, hot water, and even sheets and towels are pretty standard in backpacker places, especially in Saigon and Hanoi. So the bottom price isn't as low, but neither are the standards. You'll say "Wow" more often than "Ugh" when opening the door to your room the first time.

Expect to pay at least $10 for a shared bath double in Saigon and $12-14 when you hit Hanoi, but what you'll get for that amount is more than twice as good as a room for that price in Thailand. You'll often get A/C and free Internet at that rate and if you spend $20 or so, your room will feel like one in a real hotel—daily maid service and all.

The selection of middle range properties here varies greatly by the number of tourists. The selection is terrific in big cities, Hoi An, Sapa, and Nha Trang, for instance, but lousy in less popular areas like Danang. When you do find a true mid-range room, $40 or so will often get you all the normal hotel amenities like air conditioning, a fridge, TV, room service, breakfast, and even a pool. We got all but the pool in Hue for $20 for three, then splurged $57 per night in Hanoi for a terrific and roomy deluxe room for three that topped most Sheraton and Marriott kind of places I've been in. In between those two prices are probably 100 to choose from in Hanoi alone.

At the top end, development is proceeding at a dizzying pace and international-standard hotels (with international-standard prices) are popping up everywhere. You can easily pay more than $250 per night for a room at one of the top places if you want, but it doesn't take much effort to get a deluxe room for half that amount. Competition is stiff and getting stiffer.

If you go up north to the hill tribe areas, hotels can vary wildly in price and quality and some towns will only have one or two hotels. Just consider it part of the experience.

Airport taxi and shuttle drivers are notorious for trying to lead you to a commission-paying hotel and will try every trick known to man. It's best to book your arrival hotel in advance and pay them for an airport pickup. Start off on the right foot!

When you look at prices in this chapter a year or more after publication, keep in mind that Vietnam has some of the highest inflation in Asia and its currency bounces around 5-10% from month to month. Lodging is often priced in dollars anyway, especially if you book online, but this impacts food and transportation costs.

Food & Drink:

There are supposedly 500 traditional Vietnamese dishes, generally variations of rice or noodles with vegetables, seafood, or meat, and a wide variety of soups. You usually use chopsticks and a spoon. Vegetarian food is plentiful and cheaper, it will usually have fish sauce used as a seasoning. The cook also might think you're being silly if you complain about the pork they threw in for flavoring. Bring a phrase book and be specific if you have restrictions.

With so many good native dishes on offer, "Western" food is a crapshoot, though this is changing in the cities as tourism increases. Due to the French influence, this is one of the few Asian countries where you can get good bread. Desserts, unfortunately, are a different story unless you find a French bakery or an ice cream shop.

As a tourist and foreigner, you will still sometimes run across situations where you're expected to pay more than the locals, sometimes far more. Your bus may stop at a restaurant where there is one menu in English and one in Vietnamese—with different prices! Take some food with you on the trip if this drives you crazy, or just suck it up and pay if prices are not too inflated. Buying fruit on the street is an exercise in frustration, as you'll perpetually be overcharged. Hit the supermarket to find equal footing.

Street stall dishes are 40¢ to $1.50, and a meal in a cheap restaurant is 75¢ to $4 depending on the atmosphere and how bad they're trying to stick it to you. Restaurants that get written up in travel articles as atmospheric stops with great food will still have main dishes that are only $1 to $6 and set menus with several courses will be $5 to $12. You'd have to hit an international hotel or a restaurant catering to foreign business travelers to spend much more than $30 for two. The three of us only topped this amount twice on our visit and that was at cloth-napkin places with multiple courses and drinks.

The tea is weak, but the coffee is excellent—no instant mud here. You just have to wait for it to drip down into the cup from the metal grounds holder, which takes a while. Sodas (30¢) and mineral water (50¢ to $1 per liter-and-a-half) are expensive by local standards, but the beer here is possibly the cheapest in the world. You can get a two-liter pitcher for as little as 60¢ at a *bia hoi* (draft beer) sidewalk stall, or spend 50¢ to $1.25 for a large beer in a typical restaurant. (Yes, it's sometimes cheaper to stay drunk than to stay hydrated.) Rice wine and Russian vodka are also inexpensive, but vary greatly in quality. Foreign liquor here is about the same retail price as in the U.S.—a rarity—so you can drink your Jack Daniels or Captain Morgan's in a cocktail without breaking the bank.

One unique drinking experience here is sitting around a big earthenware jar, with two-foot bamboo straws sticking out of it in every direction. Each person sucks on mouthfuls of "*ruou can*," or cane alcohol. It is made from sticky rice, herbs, and spices, which are all heated and then left in the ground for a month to ferment.

You can enjoy seasonal fresh fruit juice in most locations, again for a price that's on par with bottled water.

The ice cream or coconut popsicles can be a welcome treat in the heat and they're not much of a splurge at 50¢ to $1 for a cone.

Transportation:

This is the area that can break your budget: it's not that public transport is costly in Vietnam, but it's so slow and unreliable that many people give up and take planes, taxis, or a car and driver.

Though it gets a bit better each year, expect antiquated equipment run by people who couldn't care less, and departure times that are wishful thinking. The average speed on the main highway running through the country is only 35 km per hour and you can't help but notice the inordinate number of repair shops (for cars, buses, and bikes) lining the roads.

A train from Saigon to Hanoi won't cost as much as a flight, but you'll have to devote an entire two days to the trip, more if there's a breakdown, and expect departures and arrivals to be late. Plan to make some overnight stops because unless you go first-class, it won't be all that comfortable either. This is a trip where it is definitely a good value to pay the premium for first-class: Hanoi to Hue is around $40 in a soft air-conditioned sleeper, or $65 on the slightly better Livitrain car, with Hue to Saigon being a tad more.

Buses that the locals take are cheap, but are often packed full and ready to break down at any minute. Plus they'll stop for anyone who looks remotely like they're interested in boarding. Most tourists that aren't on a package tour purchase some kind of tourist bus ticket that covers their whole itinerary in an air-conditioned bus, or they purchase tourist tickets for individual trips. An open tour bus ticket that will get you around most of the main stops down Highway 1 is around $50 now for a good one, but you can use it over a period of a couple weeks to three months depending on the company. A single stop journey will be $8 to $15 depending on distance. Ho Chi Mihn City to Nha Trang, for instance is around $12, as is Hanoi to Hue.

Local trains are a great value. The scenic trip from Danang to Hue, which goes through thick vegetation in the mountains and hugs the shoreline for terrific views, is only $4.

You can usually fly from Hanoi to Saigon for under $100 on Jetstar. That's on par with the train and about 1/5 of what

Vietnam Air charges, so pray they don't go under. When I was there, flights from Saigon to Danang were advertised for $55. Book ahead if it's high season because the planes are often filled and factor in baggage charges.

Once you've gotten somewhere, local transportation is cheap and easy. You can nearly always get a *cyclo* (bicycle rickshaw) ride for less than a dollar a mile with some bargaining; unfortunately these are being pushed off the roads nearly everywhere to make room for more motorbikes and cars.

Taxis are metered, though you sometimes have to push them to use it. A typical starting point is 50¢, and most around-town rides will be between $1.50 and $4. A taxi from the airport or train station to your hotel will be $5 to $14 in most spots, up to $20 in Hanoi. You can rent a motor scooter for $5 to $10 per day or rent bikes for a dollar or two, which is suicidal in the two big cities, but a nice way to get around in Hue or Hoi An.

If you can figure out the local bus system, you can get around for almost nothing: fares are about 15¢.

What Else?

•   It's a great experience to hire a combination cyclo driver and guide to take you around sightseeing. For $15 to $20 for the day for two, you're sure to get plenty of historic insight.

•   A day tour in an air-conditioned van will generally be $8 to $10 per person, often including lunch.

•   If you can get a group of people together, you can hire a four-wheel drive vehicle and driver for a week for less than $60 a day and see the picturesque hill tribe areas up north.

•   A 3-day tour of Halong Bay is around $60 to $80 per person, which includes a round-trip bus ride from Hanoi, two nights at hotels, three boat rides, and food. Similar deals are available to Sapa and south of Saigon for the Mekong Delta region at around $20 to $30 per day.

•   Admission prices to museums and attractions are reasonable, in some places quite cheap. It's not uncommon to visit a major museum and pay $1.50-$2, perhaps 50¢ for kids

12 and under. The citadel and tombs of Hue are about the most expensive attractions around, at $4 each for adults, $1 for kids. (When I visited in the late 1990s, they were $5 each—I like that trend.)

• Despite all the coastland, there are not all that many good diving and snorkeling spots in Vietnam. Save those for another place and go kayaking in Halong Bay instead. Or windsurfing in Mui Ne.

• If you're going to Bangkok earlier, you can get a cheap package deal from local agents that will include a round-trip flight and your visa for Vietnam, or you can go overland through Laos or Cambodia. Any of these options will be cheaper than getting a visa before you leave home – for instance, it's $79 Canadian to get it in Ottawa before departure, but less than $30 if you get it in a neighboring country. Vietnam allows a multiple-entry visa good for 90 days if you'll be staying longer.

• The lovely French and Chinese influenced town of Hoi An is not only a great place to visit, it is also a center for custom tailoring. Prices have risen and traffic has increased as the luxury crowd has moved in, but women can still get several outfits made for $100 or $150, including silk items. Men can get a suit made for under $80, though the quality is not as good as you can get in Bangkok.

• In Nha Trang, the legendary Mama Hahn party boat trip is no more, but neutered versions still run for under $10 a day. You get an all-day boat cruise around nearby islands that includes an amazing amount of seafood, mulberry wine, fruit, and a snorkeling stop. Or just hang out on the beach under a rented umbrella and let the beer and food come to you.

• For a little culture instead, lay out $3 to $5 and go to the water puppets show in Hanoi. Cultural performances in other cities are frequently $1.50 to $3.

• What you can get for a buck or less: a conical woven hat, a short cyclo or taxi ride, a few hours of bike rental, a bootleg CD or two, a liter or two of draft beer, a large bottled beer, a souvenir fan, a manicure or pedicure, two bowls of pho, two coffees, rental of two deck chairs and an umbrella on the beach, an hour of high-speed Internet access, three loaves of French bread.

ASIA

India

Let's first get it out of the way that India is about the wackiest place you can choose to visit. The further down the budget scale you go, the wackier it gets. It is also in the midst of massive changes, with its economy lurching forward quickly, then pulling back just as quickly by a crumbling infrastructure and a government that can't get out of its own way. If the country's economy were a train, it would be a third-class one lurching through the countryside, occasionally picking up speed before having to clear cows and make small station stops.

Even with worrying, double-digit inflation, and big increases in visitors over the past decade, India is still one of the top budget destinations in the world. But now the backpackers are joined by planeloads of "money is no object" luxury travelers and foreign business travelers trying to cash in on rising income levels. What the shoestring traveler spends in two months, the other type spends in one or two days.

"Luxury" and India seem like an oxymoron when there are cattle sharing the streets with deformed beggars and the electricity in the cities routinely goes out every day. But you will pay as much (or more) at The Four Seasons Mumbai as you will at a Four Seasons in Canada and as hard as it may be to believe, you can easily spend more than $500 per night for a standard double in Calcutta. Some of the palace hotels in

Rajasthan list rates north of $1,000 per night, and the hotspots in Mumbai will cost you as much as a night in New York City. This is not just driven by outsiders either: India has more than 200,000 millionaires and by 2016 is expected to have more than half a million.

Thankfully, you could still stuff a few essentials into a backpack, buy a budget plane ticket from Bangkok, and then travel around for $500 a month once you land. India is still full of bedraggled backpackers on a quest for something: spiritual renewal, the meaning of life, the ultimate high, love—you name it. There are still plenty of places without the means to please the moneyed crowd, and plenty of heartier travelers kicking back there taking it all in.

The Indian rupee has continued to decline the past few years and does not look likely to reverse. That's good news for those with dollars or euros, but you do have to factor in high inflation. That inflation could easily come down with more efficient distribution systems and a more open import climate, but populist forces in the government wanting to protect the current system keep striking both down.

Nevertheless, the middle class is exploding in India. This is good and bad if you're a mid-range traveler. On the one hand you've got a wider choice of places to stay than you used to have. On the other hand, they're more likely to be full because of increased domestic travel.

It has been repeatedly said that India is a "love it or hate it" destination, but like most generalizations about this large and strange land, it's not quite that simple. The poverty, poor sanitation, animal-filled streets, and a populace composed of blatant liars who love an argument can be difficult for some people to stomach. Things are mellower outside the main tourist areas and after a while you will notice a warm welcome from hospitable people who seem ready to do almost everything for you. But it takes at least two weeks to get your bearings and tune out some of the assaults on your senses. If you can handle it (and nearly six million tourists do each year), you'll be treated to fantastic sights, colorful characters, and some of the cheapest prices on the planet—sometimes you'll wonder what planet you're on!

As far as geographic variety goes, you'll find it all in India: white-sand beaches, jungles, deserts, endless plains, hillside tea plantations, and a big section of the Himalayas. The cities range from magical, princely kingdoms to colonial outposts to the teeming craziness of Bombay and Delhi. You'll experience many mental states here, but boredom won't be one of them!

There are so many highlights here that it takes months to do the country any justice. The Taj Mahal is more magical than any picture can convey, and the desert castles of Rajasthan (especially the oldest living fort in the world in Jaisalmer) are amazing sites. Some of the Himalayan towns are breathtaking, Dharamsala and Ladakh have become the real Tibet, and the trippy temples and ruins of southern India offer a whole other different experience. Most of the tourist brochure sites are in the northern half of the country, but Southern India is less touristed, friendlier, and cheaper. It also has the good beaches. Almost all the northeast states require a special area permit that must be arranged in advance, and can be quite complicated. Some disputed border areas—particularly Jammu & Kashmir—have some extra limitations and are often unsafe. Get reliable information before you plan to visit the area.

For those willing to experience the real Indian feeling, a backpacker couple can live on a budget as low as $20 per day if chilling out in Goa, Hampi, Manali, or some Kerala beach for a while. Patient hagglers can bring their costs down considerably over time. Bargaining is the norm and you should definitely learn the art of haggling, but be reasonable and keep always in mind how much a rupee is worth in relation to your money. Some nationalities have earned a bad reputation for pushing the game too far. Some economists estimate that India has one-third of the world's poor, greater numbers than in Sub-Saharan Africa. So a dollar really does mean a lot in that context.

A couple spending $40 to $60 per day can enjoy better train tickets and hotel rooms, while spending more than $100 a day for two can take some serious effort in some areas, especially in the far north or the south, away from the main tourist spots. If you have $100 per day for two budgeted for a vacation, you will not have any money worries here unless you're doing a short tourist loop of the big cities and/or are trying to stay in hotels above the 3-star level. There is a lot of seasonality to pricing in India. It's not uncommon for hotel prices to double or triple when high season hits, then drop back down in slower months. Study a guidebook carefully when making plans. Try not to spend more time than needed in business centers as costs in those can double or triple your daily expenses.

In this country, there's a government-mandated "sock it to the tourists" mentality at major sights. At the Red Fort in Delhi or the Meherangarh in Jodphur, locals pay 10 rupees (20¢), while the foreigners pay 250 rupees ($5). At the Taj Mahal in Agra, it's 20 rupees for locals, 750 for foreigners. You sometimes have to pay more to bring in a camera or to shoot video—both seeming like relic policies in the days of smartphones. Or you'll be asked to pay more for a somehow mandatory audio tour. There's no getting around it, so suck it up and pay if the attraction is high on your list. Give it a pass if it's not. In general, the less popular the site, the less it will cost. The Kite Museum in Ahmedabad is free. So is the Sulabh International Museum of Toilets in Delhi.

When the last edition of this book was going to press, Mumbai was rocked by a terrorist attack that killed over 200 people and specifically targeted high-end tourist and business hotels and restaurants. Nothing on that scale has happened since, thankfully, but sectarian violence can break out in a heartbeat in India, and it doesn't take much to overwhelm the underpaid, undertrained police force. Be aware of your surroundings and keep an eye on the local newspapers—a whole lot of them are in English and are cheap.

Speaking of religion, there's always a big battle below the surface in India when it comes to vices, especially alcohol. Bar owners in Mumbai reportedly need 20 different licenses to sell booze and up to 36 more to play music. Frequent crackdowns increase the headaches, and that's one of the more liberal states; some don't allow alcohol sales at all and others require you to enter a special bar with no windows just to have a beer. As often happens in these cases, hash and marijuana are easier, and cheaper, to come by. Since the sadhus smoke (and supposedly so did Shiva), there's not much bother about that substance.

One word you'll learn quickly in India is "baksheesh." A tip or a bribe, depending on how you look at it, is an inescapable fact of life in India. It's the main reason why the World Bank ranked India 132 on a list of 183 countries for "ease of doing business." Nearly everyone has his or her hand out. Factor this into your budget for doing anything from buying train tickets to sending a package from the post office.

Accommodation:
You can still occasionally find a bottom end room in India for $5 a night, but those are becoming increasingly rare as the locals can afford to travel more. If you're on the hunt for these, put feet on the street: many of them aren't online and the ones that are pad the price significantly. The average cheap double room costs $6 to $16 a night for varying degrees of comfort, but it depends a lot on the state and the season. You can find a nice room with a private bath in Rajasthan or the far south for $4 a person in summer, but in Delhi for that money you may have a sun-starved and grotty room with peculiar odors in Paharganj. The cities are significantly more expensive, with Mumbai and Bangalore being in the stratosphere in Indian terms—double or triple your budget there. In general, you'll do much better looking around in person than you will booking a hostel or hotel in advance. Only do that when rooms are scarce or when you first fly in. Above all, this is a place to keep your finances in perspective; sometimes an extra dollar or two a person per night can mean the difference between a dark, grubby cubicle with peeling paint, and a big, bright room with a great view. (The squat toilet is pretty tough to avoid in this range, unfortunately).

In the last few years, thanks to an economy rising 6% to 8% per year, the standards have improved a lot, but prices have, of course, increased accordingly. Owners of 350 year-old *havelis* are breaking down walls to suit Western travelers' expectations. Sometimes budget hotels and guesthouses add A/C to the rooms and then promptly double the rates. Spending a bit extra for this can be worthwhile, especially during hot and monsoon seasons.

Outside of the big cities and vacation spots, $12 to $40 per night puts you in the mid-range hotel category. For that price, you'll often get a private bath with hot water and a western toilet, a TV, A/C, and maybe room service, a balcony, or other surprises. In Goa, that price can get you a pool. Outside of the palace hotels in Rajasthan, or places where the international chains have moved in, $80 will frequently cover one of the best rooms in town. In fact, in many rural towns you couldn't spend more than $50 on a double room if you wanted to. There is a rapidly growing middle class in India, however, so expect lots of competition for mid-range hotel rooms if there's an Indian holiday or festival going on. Prices become ridiculous then and you cannot get away from crowds. Also note that hotels at the $10 per night and above range come with a graduated "luxury" tax of 5% to 10%, and some also add an extra service charge. Ask up front to avoid surprises.

India has a long history of attentive service, and it shows at the luxury level. Hotels here may have the highest staff-to-guest ratio in the world. Many of these hotels routinely top "best in the world" lists run by travel magazines. Labor is cheap, so it's not uncommon to be waited on by four people at a hotel restaurant, each responsible for a different aspect of your dining experience. Here, more than anywhere outside Africa, travelers with a hefty budget see a very different side of the country than those on a shoestring. If you can splurge once in a while for dinner or cocktails, you'll feel like you've entered a different country.

Food & Drink:

You can eat like a maniac in India, three meals a day in restaurants, and still spend less per day on food than you would buying a sub sandwich at your local deli at home. All-you-can-eat vegetarian thali meals are 50¢ to $1.50 (even less in the south) and backpacker restaurants serving "Western" food will usually cost less than two bucks per person. There's usually no point in risking your health by eating street food other than snacks (like samosas)—the restaurants are cheap. Naturally, it's mostly Indian food, but without the huge variety you see on a menu at home, unfortunately. You'll find different items in different regions. The western food on offer is usually a badly muddled imitation, but is still welcome at times.

It's best to avoid meat except in upscale hotels that cater to Westerners, or after your stomach has at least had a couple weeks to build up some immunity. If you're a vegetarian or you become one while you're here, you'll save money (vegetarian dishes and vegetarian restaurants are the cheapest) and stay healthier. After you see the butcher shops in the markets, you'll know why. Thankfully, this is one of the easiest countries in the world to be a vegetarian since a good portion of the population is as well, especially in the south.

It's pretty painless to splurge on a fancy meal now and then. If you spend $10 to $15 between you, then you'll probably have cloth napkins and waiters in formal garb as you go through three courses presented with a flourish. To spend more than that, you'd need to go to an overpriced tourist trap or a trendy eatery in Bombay, Madras, Bangalore, or Delhi. It's worth it to pay for a good meal now and then to remind you what top-end Indian food tastes like, especially in the foodie state, Gujarat. If you only eat thalis in the very cheapest places for weeks on end, it all starts tasting the same.

The British seem to hate the sweet, milky spiced hot tea (chai) served virtually everywhere, but many others love it. It's usually less than a dime a glass on the street, and it's generally a safe thing to drink because both water and milk are boiled. Bottled water is about 25¢ for a liter and sodas are a quarter. Tap water is only safe in Bombay, where it's heavily chlorinated. Railway stations and many public places (e.g. Museums), especially in large cities, offer free and safe filtered water. You can refill your bottle, save a few extra cents per day, and avoid polluting India with extra plastic bottles. The yogurt drink lassi (20¢ to 50¢) comes in many forms and will put some helpful bacteria in your stomach. The usual Western soft drinks and local versions like "Thums Up" are everywhere, and fresh lemon soda offers a fresher alternative. Good coffee is hard to find outside the cities, but is getting more prevalent each year. When it's available, it's very good thanks to Starbucks-like chains that target the new middle class. (And Starbucks just opened one in 2012.) The most popular local shop, Coffee Day, has over 100 cafes in Delhi alone. Barista and Costa Coffee are closing the gap. A cappuccino is around $1 to $1.50.

Beer prices vary drastically due to taxes: a 20 oz. bottle can be 50¢ at the bars in Goa, but can be as much as $3 in other states. The most common Indian lager is Kingfisher. Some of the states are "dry" (but tourists can get a weekly alcohol license in most of the top-end hotels) and in other states you'll have to search hard for alcohol, especially in Muslim regions.

The Indian sweets take some getting used to, but are pretty good if you buy from a decent shop (a dozen for $1). The ones sold from street carts come with a side of flies, but try the *jalebis* in Old Delhi.

Transportation:

Transportation is cheap and frequent throughout the country, though speed and comfort are a different story. Sometimes you'd gladly pay extra for an air-conditioned bus or an express train, but there's just not one available.

The 14,000-kilometer train network is quite amazing, however. It is the world's biggest employer, with 1.6 million people keeping the trains running. This is where you'll see the real India since almost 14 million people travel on the train every day. An overnight second-class sleeper can be as little as

$3, and the 17-hour trip from Delhi to Jaisalmer is around $6 for a bed. Air-conditioned first-class is roughly 2-1/2 times the price of second-class, but you get what you pay for and you'll be far less annoyed, especially on journeys that can last all night and half the day. Nobody can reach their hand in the window to grab something while you're sleeping, and vendors aren't allowed to parade through all day and night. There are actually eight different classes, of course not all available on every train, with three A/C sleeping ones. On many national routes, otherwise overbooked weeks in advance, there's a special tourist quota you need to get in the habit of requesting.

All train prices are set according to the number of kilometers. You can go 2,000 kilometers (1,240 miles) on an air-conditioned sleeper train for less than $50, including bedding. On the one-day A/C express trains ($13 from Bangalore to Chennai, for example) and on all Rajdhani Express trains, multiple meals are thrown in as well. Be aware of touts who try to resell tickets for sold out trains: the conductor is likely to check the name on the ticket and fine you, and you could probably have had the same ticket for the ordinary fare using the tourist quota.

If money is no object, you can spend $800 per night as a couple and go on the "Palace on Wheels" train through Rajasthan. Alas, for that price the view outside the windows won't get any more pleasant when you pull into a station.

Buses can be dusty, crowded hulks crammed with people and a pig or two on the roof, or can be a "luxury" bus that at least has assigned seats. Prices are comparable to the train (in 2nd non-A/C class), but the buses are more direct for some routes. As a rule of thumb, a cheap bus is a dollar for 2-3 hours, while a private bus costs 60¢ to 90¢ per hour traveled and it's unlikely you'll want to stay on board for more than 12 hours. Long distance night buses have "sleeper" options as well (usually for a 25% extra), but avoid those buses whenever possible as they are not the safest option. When the number of passengers plus the age of the bus is over 100, you have discovered the real rural India. And it's a good time to get off.

Apart from a cruise down the backwaters in Kerala, there aren't many opportunities to get around on a boat.

Internal flight prices have come down in recent years, but can still feel expensive since the main domestic airlines, Indian Airlines or Jet Airways, charge foreigners a higher price in dollars. A flight can shave days off a long trip: India is a big country. Delhi to Mumbai (Bombay) can take at least 24 hours on the train, so $65 to $120 for a flight can be money well spent if you don't have all the time in the world. Budget airlines charge the same amount for Indians and tourists so you may find better deals on those for some routes, between $40 and $70 one way. It's a very competitive market, so shop around locally.

Local transportation is generally on motorized rickshaws, though you'll find car taxis in the cities and bicycle rickshaws in some spots. In most of the major cities the cabs and auto-rickshaws have a meter, but you'll have to fight to get them to use it. Elsewhere you'll need to bargain like crazy up front to avoid getting taken to the cleaners. Ask a local first what a reasonable fare should be. There are usually enough drivers hanging around that you can end up at a reasonable price by haggling: starting from 30¢ for a short hop to $20 and up for the whole day. Prepaid taxi and auto rickshaw booths are available at major railways stations and airports with government-approved fixed rates.

Only someone with a death wish would try to rent a car here. India has one of the highest road accident rates in the world and five minutes on those roads will show you why. Note as well that the price of petrol is higher in India than in the U.S. Hire a driver ($35 - $60 per day) and agree ahead of time on what is included in the price. Then kick back and let him navigate around the sleeping cows and loaded-down auto rickshaws. If you do want to explore on your own, a motorcycle, ironically, is probably safer. You can dodge the potholes and cows easier.

City infrastructure in India has typically lagged far behind growth, but Delhi has been getting its act together and pushing through major projects. There's a high-speed rail line to the nice new airport and the fast-expanding, air-conditioned subway already carries close to two million people a day. It's planned to grow to 440 kilometers by 2020.

What Else?

• You can take a camel safari through the desert in Rajasthan for $15 to $25 per day including meals.

• Treks and white-water rafting trips through the Himalayas are available for $15 to $40 per day including a guide, lodging, and equipment. Haggle a lot, check the equipment, and reconfirm what you're getting for your money before you take off. You can even ski part of the year north of Manali.

• Drugs, especially hash, are cheap and plentiful, which is why areas like Goa and Manali are full of strung-out stoners who still think it's the age of Aquarius. There are periodic round-ups, however, usually with the goal of enhancing the incomes of local police. Overall, enforcement is lax: the god Shiva is a hashhead, so you see his hard-core followers partaking quite openly.

• You'll be asked for money all day every day, from a beggar or baksheesh seeker, from the train station to the post office, to the street corner where a barber gives you directions to a tourist site. If anyone does even the smallest favor for you, you're expected to pay a tip, even if it seems it should be part of his or her normal job. On the plus side, it's easy to get things done (including standing in line for tickets) if you're willing to pay someone and seats can magically appear on a sold out bus or train if the amount is sufficient.

• Souvenir shopping gets addictive: everything is so ridiculously cheap that you're tempted to buy out the stores. Shipping costs are quite high, so that expense can easily double the total cost if you can't carry everything home. Check the quality carefully, as there's a whole lot of shoddy stuff put out by "craftsmen" who don't seem to have much of a work ethic and there is plenty of silver jewelry on the street that isn't really silver. Best buys are (real) silver or bead jewelry, embroidered clothing (which can be custom tailored for a few extra dollars), embroidered pillowcases, sandalwood carvings, purses and bags, and shoes. Delhi offers a good selection from around the country.

• Indian-printed English-language books are $2 to $3, with beautiful coffee-table books and cookbooks available for under $10. Imported books are expensive, so go used for those.

• Don't book tours to Kashmir, Ladakh, the Thar desert or any other remote destination while in Delhi or Mumbai. Scams are quite common and you will find better deals after arrival in the area.

• Avoid mobile roaming with your regular cell phone as you can buy a local SIM card for your (unlocked) mobile for around $5, or a brand new mobile for $25. Calls and messages are then cheap: you can send 15 text messages to the US for less than a buck.

• What you can get for a buck or less: 4-8 cups of *chai*, 3-4 sodas, 4 packs of tea biscuits (cookies), 3 *masala dosas*, 40 packets of one-use shampoo, a couple of local rickshaw rides, 4 short city metro/bus rides, a cheap thali lunch or two, a rickety bike rental for a day, a movie ticket, a 100-mile train or bus ride, 5 samosas, 6 daily newspapers, a kilo of laundry, a haircut, 2 hours of Internet access, 3 *lassis*, 16 – 20 bananas, and plenty more.

ASIA

Nepal

Plenty of countries have historic monuments, miles of beaches, or pretty scenery. But nobody has mountains quite like these. If you're into hiking or white-water rafting, or just into stunning mountain scenery, Nepal is Shangri-La. Or at least it was, before the rebels and the monarchy started going at each other. Thankfully things have calmed down again lately as a power-sharing agreement looks to be working.

The Himalayas are home to 9 of the 10 highest peaks in the world and most of those peaks are in Nepal. The scenic effect is pure majesty. And with food and lodging costing about five percent of what they do in say, Switzerland, you feel almost guilty enjoying such a moving experience for so cheap.

And it's not just snow-capped, five-mile high mountains that stick in your memory. The inspiring Buddhist and Hindu temples of the Kathmandu Valley and the Newari architectural styles are magical. The people drift by awash in brilliant colors and jangly jewelry and it's hard deciding on what *not* to purchase from the local craftsmen and shopkeepers.

Like India, however, it's not for everyone. Nepal's people have about the lowest per capita income in the world, so the poverty is very real. Sanitation is deplorable in parts of the main city, and you'll constantly be aware that the locals consider you very rich. Heck, the *Indians* are considered rich by Nepali standards, kind of like the Mexicans are by

Guatemalans. But when you get out of the capital and you're hiking or rafting through nature's splendor for a pittance, you realize that Nepal has a different kind of wealth and it's hard to miss home.

Another big reason why budget travelers should consider Nepal: it looks like it has edged out its competition to become the very cheapest destination in the world for shoestring travelers. Here a single traveler can still get by on less than $10 a day without working at it very hard.

Despite the rough edges and increasing pollution, Kathmandu is a great tourist town. There are loads of interesting things to see here. Some of the medieval outlying towns, former seats of power, can really take you back in time, especially if you come after the tour buses have gone for the day.

You don't have to be a mountaineer to spend time in the mighty Himalayas. There are quite a few hikes that traverse the trails, with the most famous ones being the trek to Everest Base Camp or the Annapurna Circuit trip—one of my most memorable travel experiences ever.

One lesser-known aspect of Nepal is its wildlife. Natural parks in the lowlands are home to elephants, rhinos, tigers, and more.

Keep your eye on the news and check up on the current political situation at ground level before booking a trip to Nepal, as the whole last decade has been touch-and-go. The peace and power sharing agreement between the monarchy and the Maoists was holding as this book was going to press and the former rebels seem to have traded violence for seats in the government. Many of the old fighters have been given jobs in the army or police, or have been paid a nice sum to put away their guns and get a more peaceful job.

Hopefully it's for real, but many are worried since the constitution is still in limbo and little is getting done in their parliament. See the accompanying site to this book for good international news and information sources.

Accommodation:

In the rainy season, you can still get a bed for less than a buck in some spots and splurging three dollars will cover a spacious room with shared bath. Most hotels have solar hot water heaters; so hot showers are standard in tourist areas. Spending $4 to $10 (the latter in high season) gets you a private bath and generally better conditions, possibly a restaurant or bar. A step up to $10 to $25 rooms will include maid service, a phone, room service, and satellite TV. Most hotels have a roof deck. Other amenities are give and take: on my first trip to Nepal, in Nagarkot we had a panoramic view of the Himalayas from our cheap glass-walled room and from the airy restaurant—but the toilet was outside, down two flights of stairs!

On an independent trek through the mountains, expect just a bed and blanket, with a bathroom outside or down at the end of a long hallway. You may find the occasional solar or wood-fired hot water heater, but more often you'll skip showering for a while. You can't beat the price: a dollar or two for a room.

If you go white-water rafting, you'll be camping in most cases, although one or two higher-end companies have riverside lodges built.

You can generally get a comfortable room with A/C for $50 or less and competition is stiff from an oversupply of rooms: bargaining on site will get you a better deal than booking ahead. If you do want to be pampered, there are a handful of luxury hotels in the two main cities. They range from $75 to over $300 per night in high season—the latter being what an average Nepalese worker earns over an entire year. It takes work to spend more than $200 a night anywhere though, as in you normally would have to reserve a suite. The most expensive regular room I could find in November of 2012, in the capital, was $188 per night, buffet breakfast included.

Food & Drink:

Everything looks and tastes great in Kathmandu and Pokhara, but be careful! Just because you can order salads, crepes with cream sauce, or ice cream desserts doesn't mean you should. A large percentage of visitors get sick in Nepal, usually because they play Russian roulette with their stomachs, lulled into a false sense of security by a pretty restaurant and an extensive menu.

If you avoid tap water, raw fruit and vegetables (unless you peel them), cold milk, and food that isn't hot, you'll eat like a king or queen for a few dollars a day and stay healthy in the process. There are plenty of good restaurants in the cities and prices are overwhelmingly reasonable. Even with a few drinks there are only a handful of places in the whole country where you can spend more than $20 a person on a meal. Most of those are in luxury hotels. After all, it's more than most people who live there earn in a week. A 13% VAT is usually added and a tip of 5% to 10% is expected in tourist restaurants.

In the mountains, your food choices will be limited. You'll be eating a lot of *dal* (lentils), potatoes, flat bread, and yak cheese. Not all that exciting, but filling and hearty. Eat like a local and your food bill will be a minimal part of your budget.

One unfortunate development in recent years has been the end of cheap beer in Nepal. The beers are mostly imported brands and as the local currency has declined and ingredient prices have risen, the cost of a beer has doubled to a range of $2 to $2.50. Granted, these are big bottles, but in local terms it's an extreme extravagance. With a bottle of beer costing the same as an ounce or two of marijuana or a finger of hash, guess which kind of buzz wins out?

So, most people stick to soda, water, or tea with their meal. The varieties of tea are quite good (including mint and ginger), and generally cost less than 75¢ for a full pot.

Transportation:

Most travelers fly into Kathmandu, though it is possible to arrive overland from India or Tibet if you have the endurance.

It is also advisable to fly to Pokhara ($80 - $100) or take a luxury express bus ($12 including one meal) if you're going trekking in that area: the long public bus trip is trying otherwise.

On other routes, rugged terrain, crummy roads that get washed out every year, and buses of less-than-optimum quality all contribute to journeys straight out of a harrowing "bad trip" travel essay. And those are the express buses: don't even think about cramming into a local one. The only good things about these trips are that the scenery is usually excellent and they're super cheap.

Taxis and auto-rickshaws generally cost less than a $2 for a trip of several miles and you can rent mountain bikes for $3 to $4 a day. Hiring a car and driver for the day is a much better option than trying to drive anywhere yourself. You'll spend less anyway: from $20 to $60 a day depending on the condition of the car, whether it has A/C, and how good you are at bargaining.

In the mountains the transportation is free—your legs. Hire a porter for $3 to $10 a day depending on whether he'll also be a guide and what the accommodation choices are like. As this book went to press, the Nepali government had threatened to make guides and porters mandatory on the Annapurna Circuit, along with charging a per-day tax on the journey. After an outcry they backed off, but if it crops up again, this is going to take one of the world's iconic treks into upscale tourist range. That's kind of what happened with the Inca Trail in Peru, but at least there it was for the noble purpose of keeping a lid on crowds and raising porter standards. This one's just a money grab.

What Else?

•   Expect to pay $15 to $50 per day total for a locally arranged trek without extra frills, depending on length, accommodations, food, and the number of guides and porters. Check and recheck what you get for your money. For those in good shape, it is possible to trek a well-worn circuit like the

Annapurnas without a guide or someone to carry your bags. This brings the cost down to just lodging and food (generally $7-$15 per day). Some find this to be more comfortable anyway: you can go at your own pace and sleep in lodges, while the package tourists who paid a small fortune are on a fixed schedule and often are sleeping in tents.
• White-water rafting trips average about $30 per day, including transportation, food, and camping gear!
• Most people don't think of Nepal as a place for a safari, but there are a few excellent game reserves with ample elephants, rhinos, monkeys, and birds. You can go budget-style and see a little, or stay at a fancy lodge in the middle of Chitwan National Park and watch rhinos graze while you sip a gin and tonic.
• There are a lot of excellent bookstores in Kathmandu and this is a good place to trade in guidebooks you don't need anymore.
• Marijuana grows like a weed on the mountains and is priced accordingly. You'll be offered it daily in Kathmandu whether you want it or not.
• What to buy: rice paper books and stationary, Tibetan rugs and instruments, embroidered clothing, woven hats and gloves, wooden game sets. Buy or rent trekking gear in Kathmandu: the prices double in Pokhara.
• What you can get for a buck or less: a pair of wool gloves, a wool hat, a wooden backgammon or chess set, a handmade paper journal, two pots of regular tea, a teahouse room for two on some treks, a heaping *dal bhat* dinner, an hour of Internet access, a bicycle rickshaw ride, "Tiger Balm—mister you want Tiger Balm?"

ASIA

Asia – Honorable Mentions

The Philippines

I've only been to two countries I don't really want to go back to and one of them is the Philippines. All those islands look good on paper, but are covered with paper—literally. The word "trashed" doesn't begin to describe the littered towns and beaches, and you could almost have a countrywide scavenger hunt to find a building that's not ugly. There's so little to see and do in the cities that if you're stuck in one of them more than a day, you'll probably end up at a shopping mall. (Hey, the movies are cheap and are in English!) If you can work it out to just visit the rice-terraced mountains in north Luzon and then fly to the island of Palawan, you'll leave with a good impression. Or if you're traveling on a budget that allows for upper-end hotels with private beaches, you should also leave with a good impression. Otherwise, there are greener pastures.

It's not that this string of islands is a terrible value on its own. If you're coming here from Japan or Australia and then flying back home, it'll probably seem reasonably cheap. But compared to any of the other destinations in this Asia section, it's a raw deal. Most of the beauty here is in the lagoons and under the water, not where everyone lives. So if you are coming on a diving trip and want to just kick back on an island, it's serviceable. But only at the top end are the hotels worth remembering and service is far below the usual standard in Asia—especially compared to Vietnam. On top of that, almost nobody has good things to say about the food.

On the plus side, everyone with any education speaks English, and speaks it well. (When you make a customer service phone call from your house at night, there's a good chance you'll be connected to someone in the Philippines.) Half the population seems to be on the move at any given time, so getting from A to B is usually easy. If you catch a music show of some kind, the singing will be great. If you're a divorced man in your 50s or 60s looking for a young wife, you'll soon learn why some men your age rave about this country.

A backpacker couple should expect to pay $50 to $80 per day at the low end, but much more if spending a lot of time in the cities. A mid-range budget will be all over the map because hotel choices in this range leave a lot to be desired. Bank on $80 to $150 per day for two.

Burma (Myanmar)

After depressing decades of only the most optimistic people thinking anything would improve in Burma, finally there's some real reform. I'm still in "I'll believe it when I see it" mode, but the government is making the right moves and saying the right things. People aren't being locked up for whispering something bad about a government figure. Real elections were held in 2012 and the opposition won by a landslide. Relaxed media laws have gone from not even allowing Aung San Suu Kyi's name to be printed to pretty much taking a hands-off stance with reporters. If this all plays out well, I'll have a Myanmar chapter in the fifth edition.

If you do want to go, now is probably a pretty good time to beat the crowds. Foreign investors are salivating about the opportunities in a country starved for decent hotels and infrastructure. For now, it's dirt-cheap. In a country where the best room in Yangon, facing the Schwedagon Pagoda, lists for $140 a night, you know you're going to find plenty of bargains at lower budget levels.

Fewer than 400,000 foreigners visited Burma in 2011, and a few years from now that number could end up looking like Cambodia's a decade ago: hard to believe. If you're hardy and intrepid, dig up current info or find a guidebook researched in 2012 or later. And bring plenty of cash—the antiquated banking system is one of the first priorities for an upgrade.

AFRICA & MIDDLE EAST

Counting the island nations, there are 54 countries in Africa. Well, that was true when this book came out. One or two civil wars later, the number will probably be higher. So it's rather hard to generalize about a part of the earth that contains Morocco, Cape Verde, Ethiopia, Egypt, Mauritius, Senegal, Namibia, and South Africa. There aren't a lot of common elements in there—even skin color. Plus I'm throwing another wrench in here by including one Middle East country: Jordan. Apart from jet-setters hitting the Emirates and hearty religious souls going to not-so-cheap Israel, Jordan is the only country in the Middle East that gets more than a trickle of western tourists, so it's the only one in here.

This section is noticeably sparse, and I've tried my best to find another country that should be in here, but have come up short despite questioning a lot of travelers returning from Africa and doing a lot of research. You can indeed travel through the continent as a budget traveler, and tens of thousands of backpackers do it each year. However, I still think it takes an inordinate amount of time and effort unless you've either signed up for a package tour or plan on taking lots of flights. In either case, the costs would be well beyond the parameters of this guide. Or, you just have to be really cheerful about putting comfort aside and taking whatever the poorest region of the world throws at you.

Sure, more than half the people of Uganda live on a less than $1.25 a day, but they don't go on gorilla viewing trips and stay in jungle lodges with meals included. The bush villagers of Kenya are trying to avoid lions and keep their kids away from them, not pay the equivalent of a few years' salary to spot one.

If you are going on vacation with a good bit of money, you will take great safaris, have nice cocktails at sundown watching the hippos swim, and fall asleep under billowing mosquito nets while hearing elephants roar in the distance. You'll wake up to breakfast served on your balcony and think that this is heaven on Earth.

On a budget, it's not nearly so romantic.

This doesn't mean the continent can't be done on the cheap. After all, the local population is far from rich in nearly any country you plop down in, so your western currency goes a long way. You just need to either live like a local (manioc gruel and dirt floors) or have plenty of time and patience. You could probably travel from Cairo to Cape Town for under $30 a day if you had six months to a year and took all local transportation. If you wanted to just go to Tanzania, Kenya, and South Africa over two months, multiply that daily budget range by two or three.

Then there's the problem of the ever-shifting list of places to avoid. In any given month, about ten nations are on all the official U.S. State Department watch lists for tourists. In all fairness, that's far fewer than a decade ago and the trouble spots are less numerous each time I go to research a new edition of this book.

Trying to navigate through a region of famine, civil war, malnutrition, AIDS, malaria, despots, and a pitiful infrastructure can be trying. (Not to mention you'll eat a lot of lousy meals). Most people with that kind of fortitude have traveled many places already and don't need this book. I've only included two countries in northern Africa and one in the Middle East that cater to independent travelers and where getting from point A to point B is a simple affair to arrange. The three also have more "sights," in the tourist sense of the word, than the rest of Africa combined. With apologies to Ethiopia and now-troubled Mali, most people go to Africa for animals, natural beauty, and great music, not for great monuments or architecture.

There is a well-worn backpacker trail down the east coast of Africa, starting or ending at not-very-cheap South Africa. So if you think I'm the biggest idiot ever, head straight to the route between Kenya and South Africa by way of Tanzania, Malawi (a favorite of many), Zambia, and Mozambique. I've added that section under the honorable mentions at the end.

If you want to go somewhere for a period to volunteer or work for the Peace Corps, forget everything I've said and go straight to sub-Saharan Africa, especially if you have a medical background. Saying "they could use your help" is an understatement.

AFRICA & MIDDLE EAST

Morocco

Exotic and chaotic, spellbinding and maddening, Morocco is practically rowing distance from Europe, yet it's the closest you'll get to visions of Aladdin and *Arabian Nights*.

Unfortunately, this is no longer the cheap, undiscovered, scary-sounding destination it was when my wife and I traveled around the country in 1996, spending $6 or $8 a night for our double rooms with bath. Europeans have flooded the country with package vacationers and the number of visitors from other parts of the world has also doubled several times since then. Naturally, this has led to a rise in prices and hotels that are now more often priced in euros than dirham. On the plus side, there's more competition in the middle range, and package deals from Europe can be a steal.

This land of contradictions is still a strange place that can put you in awe but also drive you crazy. If you limit your time in the obvious tourist traps (such as Marrakech) and maintain a humorous attitude toward the touts in other areas, you'll enjoy a wealth of wonders and experiences. Delve into your guidebook and you'll find plenty of destinations where you won't be hounded: uncrowded beaches, cedar forests, rugged mountains, mystical *casbahs*, and atmospheric old towns on the edge of the Sahara. Morocco is one of the most geographically diverse countries in Africa and its people cover a wide swath as well. It is relatively easy to get away from the crowds here also since most of the package tours follow a well-worn itinerary.

You can do a camel trek through the desert, go hiking or whitewater rafting in the Atlas Mountains, play golf on interesting landscapes, or even go skiing in the winter near Marrakech. The funky beach town of Essaouira is legendary among windsurfers.

Despite the romantic "desert oasis" feel, the infrastructure and hotel networks are pretty good in Morocco and getting better all the time, apart from the grungy toilets in the cheap places that is. Some of the boutique *riad* hotels are so atmospheric you'll think you've woken up on a movie set.

Morocco is a conservative Muslim country, however, and observing common sense when it comes to modesty in deed and dress is more important here than it is in Egypt, Jordan or Turkey. It's not uncommon for your bus driver to pull over at a mosque to pray and you'll have a tough time finding a beer outside the tourist hotels. (Hashish, however, is everywhere—go figure).

This is probably the toughest country in this book outside of Latin America in terms of the English language. English is at least third on the list for most Moroccans, so learning some Arabic or refreshing your memory of that high school French will come in very handy. Otherwise you will be playing a lot of charades and pointing to pictures if you don't have a guide.

Morocco has had a reputation for being dangerous and full of touts that hassle you to death. This is especially true in Tangier (though the city is improving dramatically), so if you're coming by ferry, watch out for scams. Otherwise, the country is actually pretty safe overall and while you'll get hassled in the crowded markets of the *medinas*, most spots are not any worse than you'll find in other developing countries. In general, it helps to travel with a companion or group, and if a situation seems dodgy or you feel like you're being scammed, stand your ground and make a scene.

Some women report a higher level of harassment here than in other countries, with some describing Morocco as "like walking through a construction site all day and night" if they don't have a man with them. It's generally harmless chatter from sexually frustrated single men (and it's not as bad as in India), but it gets old fast. If you can walk around town with a mixed group or another traveler who is a guy, life is easier.

On a more positive side, interracial couples are quite common in this crossroad of cultures, so if you are one and are tired of being stared at, come here.

Craftsmanship is universally high in Morocco and you don't see nearly as much poorly made tourist drek for sale as in most other travel destinations. Even the most humble house or building is adorned in some way and craftsmen (and women) take great pride in their work. You could practically furnish and decorate a whole house with what's on sale in the craft markets—at a tiny fraction of what the designer boutiques are charging in the big cities at home, and it would look designer-chic fabulous.

The Moroccan currency, the dirham, moves closely in step with the Euro these days, so for Americans it can get expensive fast when the euro is strong, especially at the mid-range level, where Europeans go about feeling like the whole country is on sale. Many boutique riad hotels are priced higher than comparable properties in Spain and Portugal in high season. This is a country where booking a package deal ahead of time can cost far less than booking a hotel independently for places priced $50 or so a night and higher.

A couple can scrape by on as little as $40 a day in Morocco, but it's not easy if you're moving around much or doing any activities. Two people sharing a basic room should realistically expect to spend $50 to $80 per day here unless they take long breaks between intercity travels and self cater some. Singles should expect $35 and up unless they're staying put or doing some camping. Midrange travelers should be reasonably comfortable at $80 to $150 per day for a couple, but this is a place where spending a bit more on nicer hotels is worth it if your budget permits—you get a lot of beauty for your money.

For just a little bit more than that, you can get on an organized tour with a company like G Adventures and have a guide taking care of all the logistics. You just write a check and go. I'm not normally a big advocate of that, but here it makes a lot of sense economically and it's the route I'd take if doing something like an Atlas Mountains trek.

Most nationalities get a 90-day stay automatically, so take your time otherwise. You'll enjoy it more on a local pace and will spend far less per day.

Accommodation:

The very bottom end of the scale here means camping ($3 to $7 each) or finding one of the few youth hostels ($8 to $20 each for a bed). Or a guesthouse roof, which can go for as little as a euro in some remote spots if they know you'll be eating in their restaurant. A cheapie room in a basic cold-water hotel starts at around $9 in the villages and averages $12 to $35 in the cities. To get a private bath with hot water, you'll pay at least $14 and more often $25 to $40. Triples and quads are often available, so a group traveling together can cut down the costs by sharing. Some of the hotels are dives, but some are romantic red mud buildings that seem to have jumped straight out of a scenic film. In the middle range, $30 to $70 will usually get you a government-rated, clean hotel with a TV, air conditioning, a restaurant, a furnished common room terrace, maybe a swimming pool, and perhaps some gardens or a tennis court.

For $75 to $150 a night you can get a beautiful room in a historic building that will truly make you feel like you're in Morocco, complete with Moorish arches, beautiful lighting, and plush sitting areas. At the top end, demand from Europeans has pushed up prices across the board, so research carefully before booking. There are a few internationally renowned hotels and impeccably restored riads where rates *start* at $400 per night. Even in tourist centers, that's seldom more than the top two or three: most are $200 or less.

Outside of the luxury ones, most hotels offer free Wi-Fi or shared computer terminals, so it's easy to check e-mail or make a Skype call.

Cheap hotels are priced in local currency or euros, but above a certain point they're all priced in euros only unless you book from home in a different currency. Booking ahead can be worthwhile in the main attraction areas, especially in you visit when the French and Spanish are on vacation, filling up all your first choices. Having to settle for your second or third choice can mean paying more than you were hoping, so plan ahead for Fez, Marrakech, Chefchouan, Essaouira, Casablanca, or Tangier.

Food & Drink:

The overall variety of food here is better than most people expect, though some restaurants will offer only three or four set meal choices. Dinner is often served late and takes forever to cook; take a deck of cards or have plenty to talk about while you wait.

As in most Muslim countries, the food can be a vegetarian's nightmare. If you eat with a local family, you could be served five courses—all of them featuring meat! Couscous is the national dish, but you'll have to eat in a tourist restaurant to get a meatless version.

Street foods like meatball or falafel-type sandwiches start at a dollar and a full meal at a simple stand will usually cost less than $4. Set restaurant lunches are $4 to $8. The locals don't eat out too much, so most restaurants outside the marketplaces are for tourists and dinner is on Spanish time, especially in the north. In some towns, street food or a hotel restaurant will be the only choices. Consequently, you can find some badly interpreted western food that will make you wish you'd just ordered a local stew and salad. The French left an excellent legacy in terms of bread and pastries and both are quite cheap. Breakfast can be heavenly if you're into a sweet start to the day.

Most of the mid-range hotels offer free breakfast, which is usually filling and healthy: grains, crepes, yogurt, juice, and fruit (like the delicious local dates).

For a splurge, there are some restaurants catering to tourists that are worth checking out for the atmosphere. For $30 and up, a couple can get a three or four course meal with a couple of beers or glasses of wine. It's not hard to find a place to spend $50 each in the cities here: some of the restaurants are very upscale. The most common drink is sweet mint tea (50¢ for a big glass or a little over a dollar for a pot), but bottled water and soda are easy to find.

There are three kinds of beer and wine from three distinct districts. Finding any of them, however, takes a lot of work unless you visit a tourist hotel bar or tourist restaurant, especially outside the main cities. Expect to pay $1.75 to $4 for a beer in a bar or restaurant. Liquor stores are set up in a way that makes you feel like you're entering a bootlegger's secret store during prohibition. You can dry out in more ways than one in Morocco.

You will drink a lot of water here, especially if you come during the summer. You will spend a small fortune and create a new garbage dump with your name on it if you buy bottled water the whole time. Bring a purifier.

Transportation:

You may be hassled a lot on the streets of Marrakech or Tangier, but at least the getting away is easy. The road and rail networks are surprisingly good and reliable, as long as your schedule is flexible.

Second-class train tickets get you an air-conditioned sleeper seat in a 6-person compartment. first-class train tickets aren't really worth the premium: the air conditioning is not any more reliable and the main difference is the amount of cushioning on the seats. You can get off mid-trip for up to 5 days to break up a long journey. Short trips are usually $4 to

$8 and longer jaunts run $10 to $40. A second-class train from Casablanca to Marrakech, or Marrakech to Fez, runs a shade less than $10, double that for first. A first-class train ticket tops out at about $60 for an overnight sleeping compartment from Tangier to Marrakech (9.5 hours), with the second-class one being $21.

Buses are a mixed bag and you don't always get what you pay for. Competition is good on the standard routes, so you can get a nice air-conditioned trip from Marrakech to Fez, for example, for about $18. Most trips run $4 to $30, depending on comfort and distance. For remote locations, you may be stuck on a dusty heap crammed with dusty passengers. One annoying oddity in Morocco is the luggage charge, which is an additional 75¢ to $2 fee tacked on just to throw your bag in the compartment underneath.

City taxi trips range from about $1 to $10 depending on distance and your bargaining skills, but a cab from an airport to your hotel in Casablanca can top $30. You can take share-taxis over long distances for about double the price of a bus— which for a short jaunt is insignificant anyway. Expect an old Mercedes with a few hundred thousand miles on it, but you can rent the whole thing as a group and go from Marrakech to Casablanca for only $70 or so total. Rental cars start at around $45 per day for something very basic.

Getting to or from Spain on a ferry will cost $28 to $40.

What Else?
•   A former King loved golf, so the courses here are excellent. Greens fees aren't the bargain they used to be, running $40 to $90. But hey, you pay a shade more and a caddy will carry your bag.
•   Morocco was never invaded by the Turks or Romans and there has been a long, unbroken royal succession. The historic architecture is all quite intact.
•   If you get sick, don't sweat it. Doctors make house calls for $30 to $40.

• When you get up the energy to experience the grand bazaars and verbally wrestle with the touts and shopkeepers, look for nice soft leather, wood carvings and chess sets, copper, brass, jewelry, and stoneware. Be careful buying carpets unless you know what to look for: the cheap ones won't last. Good ones generally start at $150. Bargain hard for everything, but take your time and keep it friendly to get the best deals.

• Shipping charges in Morocco are hefty and the post offices are so slow and inefficient that you may feel like you're being filmed for a comedy skit. Take your things with you if you are returning home.

• What you can get for a buck or less: a pot of mint tea, two liters of bottled water, two glasses of fresh orange juice, two pastries, a street food sandwich, four postcards, three city bus tickets, a short taxi ride, a kilo of oranges, three loaves of bread, a quarter kilo of dates, an hour of Internet access in a café.

AFRICA & MIDDLE EAST

Egypt

The "Land of the Pharaohs" is one of the best travel values imaginable. Where else can a couple spend day after day walking through some of the greatest treasures and monuments in our planet's history for as little as $20 a day?

In the US or Australia, the word "historic" applies to something from a few centuries ago at most, in Europe maybe a thousand years ago. If something's "old" in Egypt, it's from a few thousand years BC. The Great Pyramids are only the start: many other collections of impressive ruins stand by the Nile, with Luxor, Aswan, and Abu Simbel getting the lion's share of the visitors.

But the Arab Spring hit Egypt in a big way in 2011 and as this book went to press, there were still a lot of questions about how the future would play out. What will a Muslim Brotherhood Egypt be like? How well will the tourism infrastructure and monuments be maintained? How tolerant will a new regime be about casinos, nightclubs, and bars? What will happen to religious freedom and tolerance? Huge protests were a regular affair at the end of 2012 as the new president looked to be grabbing more power and weakening the judiciary.

All the questions and negative news have sharply reduced the number of tourists in Egypt, so a country that was already a bargain is a buyer's market, especially for hotels. If you go, merchants will be very glad to see you and you'll be able to find historically great deals on everything.

Transportation is cheap and most destinations are either along the Mediterranean (beach resorts and historic Alexandria), the Nile (Cairo and the buildings of the Pharaohs), or the Sinai Peninsula—home to some of the best diving and snorkeling in the world. The only real off-the-beaten-track destinations are the oases in the desert. For most of the population, Egypt is the Nile and the Nile is Egypt. If you were going to go on a group tour somewhere, this wouldn't be a bad place to do it. Prices are ridiculously cheap and in places like Luxor, you'll need to tour the tombs with some kind of group anyway. With business way down, tour companies are throwing out crazy cheap prices or throwing in lots of extras to get you to sign up.

Cairo can be overwhelming, but it's worth spending some time to see the sights, especially the famous Egyptian Museum.

Shopping in the local bazaars can be fun, but be prepared to be hassled to death, whether you want to buy or not. Most of the time it's the latter: the souvenirs are pretty cheesy and the quality is often not very high in places where tourists congregate.

Women need to dress conservatively outside the Sinai and life will be a lot easier if not traveling alone. If you have a wedding ring and a real or imagined husband, your suitors will be a lot less persistent.

Since the Arab Spring revolt, the exchange rate has been on a slow but sure decrease in value and was 6.1 to the dollar as this book went to press, up from 5.6 in 2009. So if your own currency is up against the dollar, you'll do even better.

A single traveler could scrape by on $20 a day here. A backpacking couple that's not skipping attractions can expect to spend $30 to $50 per day in Egypt, a bit more if on the move every day. Chilling out in Dahab for a while will bring down the average. The middle range is a good value in Egypt, with cheap transportation and plenty of pretty hotels for the price of a roadside motel at home. Budget $50 to $100 per day for a couple if you plan on always having an air-conditioned room with amenities. This will get knocked out of whack when it's visit-the-pyramids day. Admission in Giza is a steep $33 each and you get tickets for the whole shebang, with no discount for enduring 50 or more shouts of, "Hello, camel ride?" "Mister, postcards? Camel hair blanket? Perfume for the lady?"

Accommodation:

Expect to pay $3 to $8 for a hostel bed or $4 to $10 for a cheap hotel room in most of the country. These are generally spartan rooms with basic services. Hot water will be hit or miss, but in a climate that feels like the inside of an oven, you probably won't care. In the southern towns, prices above $7 will often include air conditioning, essential when the afternoon mercury hits 115 degrees. Western toilets are the norm, though you may run into a squat toilet now and then in the cheapest places.

A good hotel room with private hot-water bath, A/C, and TV starts at around $16 for a double, with those tagged as being a "luxury hotel" usually listed at $35 to $90, even in Cairo. You can nearly always find a 3-star hotel for under $40 per night, often including at least one meal, and every town has dozens of nice hotels under $80. The glut of rooms at the mid and high level has created plenty of bargains, even at the international chains. Pull up Egyptian cities on any booking engine website and you'll have plenty to pick from at prices that will make you do a double-take. In Luxor, it's common to find a Sofitel, Sonesta, Le Meridien, and Sheraton going for less than $80 a night, so most indie hotels are half that.

At the top end, unless all the Saudi oil princes and their entourages are in town, luxury hotel rooms are far below the world average. Apart from the Four Seasons, you can usually find a true luxury room in Cairo or near the pyramids for well under $250 a night. Competition is even more intense in the Red Sea resort area of Sharm el-Sheikh, where a 2005 bombing (affecting mostly Egyptians) and more recent spats between Islamists and the government altered the area's image as a safe haven. Shop around a bit and you'll be amazed at how far your dollars or euros will go here for vacation.

Food & Drink:

Nobody comes to Egypt for the food. In general, it's a bland counterpart to that of its neighbors, with most meals being some combination of chicken, rice, *fuul* beans, pita bread, and pasta. Egyptians don't eat out all that much and when they do, it's dinner at 9:00 or later in the evening. The budget traveler's staple food is *kushari*, which is a flavorful and filling combination of noodles, rice, black lentils, fried onions, and tomato sauce. Apart from this and the ubiquitous falafel, vegetarians will have somewhat limited choices and everyone else will encounter mystery meat along the way (I'm sure I ate camel at least once while I was there, maybe a pigeon or two as well).

Restaurant meals are one to four dollars, although you can spend much more if you go for higher-end tourist spots. An elaborate dinner with a belly dancer can be a fun splurge, though most of the food will be Lebanese rather than Egyptian. Street stall food is 25¢ to $1.50 per person, with a bottle of soda averaging less than 40¢.

In the tourist areas, you can find pale imitations of western food and the odd fast food joint. Stella beer is a rather soapy looking concoction, but it's a welcome sight on a hot day, which is every day here. A bottle of so-so wine is $3 to $6 if you can track one down. Hard liquor is expensive and very difficult to buy for carryout; you must go to the equivalent of a duty-free shop with your passport in hand. Alcohol access could get tougher in the future if the Muslim Brotherhood's more radical members get their way.

You'll need lots of liquid. You can supposedly drink the local water in the cities, though I wouldn't try it on day one. Bottled water is cheap and easy to find, though you'll be doing the environment a big favor by bringing a purifier: you go through a *lot* of water in Egypt, like a gallon a day. You can nearly always find fresh juice for sale on the streets.

Transportation:
Getting around to the main centers along the Nile is a bargain. The 10-hour train ride between Cairo and Luxor can cost as little as $6 in air-conditioned second-class, $15 to $20 in first-class. If you want a private first-class berth for two, you can do that for $50. Shorter trips are often just a dollar or two. The buses are even more economical and usually faster (but mainly due to suicidal drivers). You can get to most anywhere from Cairo on a standard bus for less than $8, or pony up three or four more dollars and go first-class on main routes. Share taxis from town to town are a good deal, from 30¢ to a few dollars.

Internal flights used to be ridiculously expensive, but apparently Egypt Air got tired of flying empty planes and domestic flights are sometimes as low as $35.

Subways and trams in Cairo average 15¢. A minibus to the Pyramids is also 15¢, while a taxi there is around $3 to $8, depending on bargaining skills. Try to ask around about fares and arrange a price before getting in a taxi. The drivers all seem to have gone to the same acting class. They routinely avoid committing to a price up front, then try to bluster and bully you into paying an inflated fare upon arrival. (Not too smart since you're already there!) After a few times of this it's humorous, but kind of disconcerting at first.

Avoiding these types, you can hire a car and driver for the day for $25 to $50 nearly anywhere in the country.

Bicycles can be rented for $2 to $4 per day.

As for renting a car, don't. Egyptians have a justified reputation as some of the worst drivers on the planet. They also have some odd superstition that causes them to drive around at night without turning on their headlights. Forget terrorist attacks: driving a car in Egypt is how you are most likely to die on foreign soil!

What Else?
• You can enter the Egyptian Museum in Cairo-one of the world's biggest and greatest—for around $10, less with a

student card. (You'll pay another $16 to get into the mummies room—it costs some bucks to keep those guys preserved!)
• Most souvenirs are for kitsch value only, but you find nice wall hangings, scented oils, clothing, silver jewelry, and brass items. The inlaid mother-of-pearl chess and backgammon sets can be a good buy if you inspect them carefully.
• Despite a long history of being home to traveling merchants, Egyptian vendors seem to be terrible businessmen. They'd rather give up a huge sale than to back down on a ridiculously pumped-up price. Usually it's best to stay calm, take a walk down the block, and try to find someone who looks like he has a family to feed.
• A felucca sailboat trip on the Nile for a few hours will cost $2 to $5 dollars and a 3-day trip from Aswan to Edfu can easily be haggled down to as little as $10 per person, inclusive of food, if you can get a group of 6 to 8 people together. Besides being easy on the budget, this is a relaxing experience and a great way to see life on the country's main artery.
• What you can buy for a buck or less: a beer, a few glasses of fresh-squeezed juice, a cheapo papyrus painting, a cheesy amulet with your name in hieroglyphics, three falafels, two bowls of kushari, some monument admissions, at least five bus or subway rides in Cairo.

AFRICA & MIDDLE EAST

Jordan

Jordan can't catch a break. You almost feel like dollars spent there should be tax deductible as a charity contribution. Sandwiched between Israel, Syria, and Iraq, they get punished on the world tourism stage even when they sit there quietly and do nothing to scare people off.

Jordan's proximity to three hotspots (and extreme Saudi Arabia) is certainly not something that can be overcome with glossy brochures from the Ministry of Tourism. However, anyone who has been there will tell you that it was a highlight of his or her travels. The people are some of the friendliest and most hospitable you'll run across, no matter where you're from. While it's relatively easy to get around, you won't be running into throngs of other tourists at every turn. Most people find Amman to be one of the most pleasant and civilized cities in Asia. (For one thing, cars actually stop for pedestrians).

It would be worth it to come here just to see Petra, which many people do as a short add-on to an Egypt trip. Admission is now on par with a trip to Disney World though, making it the most expensive park in the world besides the Galapagos (and even more on a per-day basis.) You'll pay a minimum of $71 for a one-day ticket, or an appalling $129 if you're on a one-day tour from Israel or a cruise ship in Aqaba. There are no discounts for anyone except children under 15, including students. (If you're Jordanian, however, you pay $1.50.) Once inside, apart from a few drink stands, the monuments stand as they have for centuries. The place is huge: miles upon miles of buildings and tombs carved into the rocks, with some requiring some serious hiking to get to. You can easily spend two or three days hiking and exploring—and that's the only way to make the admission seem anywhere close to reasonable. A three-day ticket is $86.

Petra is not the only attraction however. There are a lot of historic mosaics in Madaba, the excellent Roman ruins at Jerash, and a circuit of "desert castles" outside Amman. Many people also hike or take a desert safari around Wadi Rum—a desert canyon where much of *Lawrence of Arabia* was filmed.

Then there's the Dead Sea. This bizarre body of water, below sea level, is so salty that nothing lives in it and you can't sink. You can swim, relax on the beach, or slather Dead Sea mud on your body—something you'd pay lots of money for at a chic spa.

Prices here are not as cheap as Egypt, but are in many ways a better value. The food is better, for one thing. Transportation is a good value, with a bus ride from Petra to Aqaba only costing a few dollars. Plan on $25 to $40 per day if you're alone unless you're staying for weeks, $35 to $70 per day for a budget couple. Mid-range travelers will do okay on $70 to $120 per day for a couple. A lot of this variation depends on how long you're staying and how much you cram in. If you come for four days and spend two of those in Petra, your daily average will be far higher than someone who stays a few weeks and chills out in one place for a while. A good Wadi Rum excursion will be $50 to $80 a person per day. If you rent a car part of the time, which makes a lot of sense because of the small area to cover, that will add at least $40 per day to the budget.

The Jordanian dinar currency is tied to the U.S. dollar, so it remains stable at .70 or .71 to the dollar.

The traditional travel circuit used to be some combination of Egypt, Jordan, and Israel, with a trip to Syria thrown in for some. You could do all of this overland before, but the situation in Israel has deteriorated further with the Fatah/Hamas split and moving freely between all these countries is not a current reality. Syria is now a no-go zone. So check out other transportation options, but you should still be able to get here from Egypt by boat or a short hop flight regardless of what's happening politically.

Prices in Jordan are especially volatile because of the fluctuations in the U.S. dollar and the price of oil. Take everything in here as a rough guide—and do the same with any guidebook, no matter how current it may be.

Accommodation:
Cheap hotels are nothing to write home about, but are generally clean and reasonably comfortable. You can find a dorm bed in most spots for $4 to $10. Often you'll be assigned a cot or mat on the roof! You can camp in some areas and if you go on a desert safari, that's what you'll be doing. (Keep in mind it gets very hot in the day but can get cool at night). You can usually find a double room for $10 to $24.

The mid-range hotels here are a very good value, with a three- or four-star hotel being $35 to $80, even in Amman, where there are typically 25 or more hotels under $50 a night on the booking sites. Decent hotels here are pretty relaxed for the Middle East. Most have a bar or disco and you can often get a beer with your meal.

Luxury hotel prices are in flux depending on which neighbors are fleeing trouble in their own country. Still, this is a place where you can stay at the best place in town for $200 or less almost anywhere. There are some really special hotels around Petra. Since you'll probably only be here a night or two anyway, this is a good place to splurge. The stunning Movenpick near the ruins there is routinely less than $150 per night.

Food & Drink:

Food in Jordan is more Middle Eastern than in Egypt, with fuul beans being a standard and baba ghanoush and hummus everywhere. Other standards of the region, such as schwarma and falafel are here in force. You can also find a sort of a mini pizza containing meat, cheese, potato, or herbs and olive oil for about 50¢.

Other street food is often 70¢ or less and meals range from $1.50 to $4 each at the low-end restaurants. Outside of the very top hotels, you can get a very good (and very filling) multi-course meal in a reasonably nice restaurant for $7 to $12 each.

A sweet, thirst-quenching lemonade is less than 20¢ and fresh juices are 40¢ to 50¢. Beer and wine are two of the few things that are cheaper in neighboring Israel. Beer is heavily taxed in Jordan, making it $2 to $3 per bottle. (Meanwhile, a pack of cigarettes is a third of the price—welcome to the Middle East!)

Transportation:

Figure $3 to $4 per hour on a proper bus, less on a minibus that makes a few more stops. This is not a very big country, so four or five bus trips usually covers most of the itinerary. Unfortunately, there are very few budget tours set up, so visiting some areas requires either a good knowledge of the local bus options or a car rental for a day or two. (If you get stuck at the Dead Sea, for instance, you'll pay a pretty penny to spend the night).

A bus from the airport to downtown Amman is less than five bucks, but a cab ride can cost you $30. Taxis within the capital are actually metered, which is a concept you don't see often in this book. You can get across Amman for under $5.

What Else?

•   Your visa fee used to depend on what your home country charged Jordanians to come there. It is now standardized at $15 to $35 depending on length of stay.

•   Bargaining seems a bit half-hearted here, and you won't be quoted prices that are three times what the real value is. You can knock a little off, but there's a lot less work on both ends. Shopping is just so-so anyway: buy here only if you're on your way home or if this is the only stop.

•   If you get a group of people together instead of just buying a spot on a tour, you can do a good overnight Wadi Rum canyon excursion for about $30 to $40 each, including meals and equipment.

•   There is some good diving in the Gulf of Aqaba, but to really see anything from Aqaba itself, you'll need to go out on a boat trip.

•   What you can buy for a buck or less: a stack of warm pita bread, a schwarma, a half kilo of cookies, a couple fresh juices, two bowls of fuul, three or four city bus rides, a couple cups of Turkish-style coffee.

Africa - Honorable Mentions

The Eastern Route: Kenya, Tanzania, Zambia, Malawi, Mozambique

There's a lot to see and do in Western Africa, but it is quite expensive to travel through—beyond the scope of this book. Making it worse, some countries there have yet to be connected to the Internet except by very expensive satellite service. And the radicals now controlling Mali have banned playing or even listening to music. Mali!

Botswana and Namibia have worked hard to lure smaller, wealthier crowds in order to keep the environment intact where wildlife congregates. A worthy and noble goal, which actually seems to be working, but it means you'll need to wait until you've got a few grand to throw around on vacation before you spend some time in that region.

Costs in South Africa fluctuate greatly depending on exchange rates, but when their currency is strong you'll pay as much as you would in many developed countries. At least a dozen countries are generally off limits due to civil wars or other disturbances. Madagascar is relatively cheap on the ground, but getting there is not.

Besides the countries covered in depth already, that leaves East Africa, which is the area most trod by travelers on a budget. Despite it being a somewhat well worn path, easy it is not.

If there's one consistency throughout most of Africa, it's that public transport is universally derided as ranging somewhere between "quite uncomfortable" and "excruciating." It's slow, dusty, crowded, and hot. On the east coast stretch of Africa, however, enough travelers are passing through that some semblance of a parallel transportation system has developed, with backpacker shuttles plying some routes. There is a better network of places to stay as well. Even the most charitable guidebooks stop short of saying there are comfortable budget hotels in much of Africa, but on this route, there's a better chance of getting a room that won't make you cry.

The universal problem is that there is a top end, with luxury hotels and safari lodges, and a bottom end, with shabby guesthouses that are poorly run. In the vast middle ground, there are not many choices unless you're on an organized tour. Expect to scrape by on as little as $15 a day if you aren't on the move all the time and are not spending many of your days on adventures. Few people do this. Moving up the activity or transportation scale, $25 to $35 for one or $40 to $60 for two is more common, depending on the length of time in Africa. The more you see and do, the more it will cost, so many couples find they have trouble doing what they want to do on less than an average of $50 a day.

Budgets are primarily higher here because people don't come to Africa to see monuments, museums, or lovely cities. They come here to see wild animals, view natural wonders, and maybe climb Kilimanjaro. For safaris (usually Kenya or Tanzania) and treks up Kilimanjaro, any budget below $100 per day almost guarantees a lousy trip. At that level, costs are being cut to the bone and guides and porters are going to be poorly paid. Budget $150 per day and up if you really want to have "the experience of a lifetime." Then there are temptations for scuba diving, the trip to Victoria Falls, rafting on the Zambezi River, and plenty more. In Mozambique and Mali, however, you can make up for it by just kicking back on the ocean or the lake and grooving on some great music.

Costs for transportation and food also come into play, however. Most travelers end up taking at least one or two internal flights to avoid especially long overland trips. The staples of corn mush, root vegetables, and fatty meat can get old fast as well, so some splurging now and then on better meals should be factored into the budget. The point is, Africa can be a fantastic, mind-altering experience, but just because the countries are poor doesn't mean the travel prices are rock bottom. Come here with a bigger budget than you would for North Africa or Southeast Asia. This is also a continent where going on a group tour can make a lot of sense. You may find you can do a trip with the likes of G Adventures or Intrepid for not much more than you would spend trying to work it all out on your own.

EUROPE

Everybody wants to go to Europe it seems. From college students on summer break to retirees packed in bus tours, a trip to Europe seems to be the one obligatory overseas trip. Whether it's the lure of ancestry or the desire to see historic civilizations, it's a powerful pull. Which is fine if you have plenty of bucks to spare or don't mind sharing every experience with 50 to 500 other people.

Otherwise, spending a couple of weeks in most parts of Europe is going to hit your credit card in ways you never imagined. If you're a budget traveler, you'll be staying in dorm rooms you had to book in advance, eating lots of bread and cheese, and having to pass on a lot of attractions and restaurants that you can't afford. If you're American or Canadian, prices will seem to fluctuate between outrageous and insane. Traveling here is like shopping at Tiffany's: you won't leave the place without laying out more than you had planned.

Whatever is happening with exchange rates and the euro, Western Europe is pricier than most other parts of the world— only Japan is consistently more expensive. Taxes are higher, gasoline is twice as expensive, and there are plenty of protectionist policies that keep farm and labor costs high. These things all trickle down into everything you spend money on.

In parts of Eastern Europe, however, you can still find that European experience without spending European rates. You also won't feel stuck in a land of chain stores and fast food joints in the cities. (And if you must go to Western Europe, rural Spain and Portugal are the best values.)

Unfortunately, as new countries join the EU, their prices move closer to the mean, especially in the cities. I added Slovakia to this edition and kept Romania in, but prices went up in both as soon as the champagne corks popped during the EU membership celebrations.

The other factor driving up prices throughout Europe is the "Ryanair effect." As soon as a city, no matter how obscure, starts getting flights in from the likes of easyJet and Ryanair, planeloads of new vacationers flood in, arriving on 30-euro promotional fares. Often these visitors are just in for a weekend of debauchery, so they spend indiscriminately and form a new baseline for local business owners. Remember, every action, like cheap airfares, has an equal and opposite reaction. There's always a tradeoff...

For over 35 years, the pioneering travel resource for meaningful work, living and study abroad.

EUROPE

Slovakia

Slovakia is not as cheap as Bulgaria, Romania, or Hungary, but it does offer better values than most of the rest of Europe, plus you get the advantage of feeling like a pioneer. While Prague and Budapest see millions of visitors each year, Slovakia subsists on a few tourism scraps in the way of river cruise visitors to Bratislava and...little else.

This is a shame because the country really has a lot to offer and Košice has one of the most pleasant historic centers you could wish for. Here you can eat well, drink well, and find plenty of sights to marvel over at a fraction of the cost of the countries to the west. Without the loads of tour buses and big groups led by someone with a megaphone or a flag, here you can relax on vacation and not have to work so hard at taking a photo without mobs of people.

Most people don't know the first thing about this country and half get it mixed up with Slovenia, but think of it as the right half of old "Czechoslovakia." As such, it has much of what you would expect to experience on the other side of the border—without the price inflation of Prague and with good ole euros as your currency.

It's the country's participation in the single currency that keeps it from being as cheap as the other three European countries in this book, all with their own money still. Locals say prices took a hike the week the euro went into effect and never went back down. It makes for some interesting cross-border trade in the north: when the euro is weak, the Poles come across the border to load up on alcohol. When the euro is strong, the tide goes the other direction.

The main attractions here are outdoor ones, so coming in the dead of winter isn't a great bet unless you want to take advantage of relatively cheap skiing and snow sports in the High Tatras Mountains. From April through Autumn, you can hike in those mountains, explore castles, and see interesting historic cities. Adventure activities go from tame to wild, with a lot of unpopulated areas to explore on foot, by bike, or on river raft. There are also a lot of caves in this region, including one where you can ride a boat "on the River Styx" and come out a tunnel at the end in Hungary.

If you haven't gotten your fill of monasteries in Bulgaria or Romania, there are dozens of gorgeous ones here to check out, as well as some historic wooden churches and several UNESCO World Heritage sites. (Remember that the borders have shifted a lot in this region from a century ago: much of what's in Romania or Slovakia now used to be in Hungary—and sometimes vice-versa.)

You'll seldom pay more than six euros for admission to anything, and usually it's more like two. Transportation is reasonable, but not all that well set up for English speakers. There's not much of a backpacker infrastructure or a network of fluent English speakers, so this is a country where I would definitely advise carrying a guidebook—and a phrase book. Or suck it up and go on an organized tour if you can find one. It'll probably start in Bratislava, as there are almost no domestic agencies elsewhere. I had two English-speaking guides in the eastern part of the country when researching an article and supposedly that was half of the total number registered!

Try to stay out of trouble here: the World Economic Forum ranks the Slovakian judicial system 140th out of 144 countries they track.

Accommodation:

As mentioned, not many backpackers make it to Slovakia. Apart from neighboring Hungarians and Poles, not many travelers period. So outside of the capital, there's not the bustling backpacker infrastructure you find in the northern Czech Republic or Budapest, with dozens of hostels to choose from and day trip tours going out regularly. So lodging tends to be a better deal for mid-range travelers: almost nothing is more than $125 per night except a smattering of international business chain hotels. It's far easier if you're a couple, not a single, as hostels are rare. Camping is easy and cheap and around the hiking areas you can rent a simple mountain hut for two for under 10 euros/$13.

Camping at many national parks is $8 for one person with a tent, $12 for two. Mountain hut bed rentals generally run $6 to $10 per person. Sometimes shared, sometimes private doubles.

A hostel bed in Bratislava is rather high because of limited competition. Figure on $17 to $25 per person. Often a couple is better off at a 2- to 4-star hotel or pension. That averages $26 to $70 double throughout the country, usually including breakfast. Sometimes you can find an apartment or house for four with kitchen for $60 to $90 per night. Less in rural areas: there are a lot of empty houses in Slovakia because the owners are working in Western Europe somewhere to make more money.

At the high end, it doesn't cost much to splurge. The best hotel in Košice is often listed for $120 or less for a standard double. In Bratislava, there are typically 30 or 40 hotels for $60 or less double, but only a few listed for more than $150.

Food & Drink:

The best deals in Slovakia are on what you consume: restaurant food, wine, and beer especially. This is a country where you can still get a big multi-course lunch and a glass or two of good wine or a great beer for less than US$10. A soda can cost more than a beer or wine, as can coffee. You can drink the tap water.

You'll seldom leave the table hungry. The local cuisine is hearty and filling. Think sheep cheese dumplings, roasted pork, big bowls of pasta, and fried cheese. Maybe with a side salad that has extra cheese, and a plate of bread and butter. Plus some peppers in olive oil and some cheese for good measure. Apart from the odd Spanish oranges and other imports, it's mostly local.

A set meal 3-course lunch is usually $3 to $8. If ordering individual items, soups are commonly $1 to $2.50, main dishes $1.50 to $6. If you're in a place you can cook, a kilo of seasonal produce is often 75¢ to $2, 100 grams of local cheese is 40¢ to $2, and rolls or baguettes are 20¢ to 90¢ each.

There's not a whole lot of street food here unless you get into a Roma neighborhood. For the locals it's generally fast food, a real restaurant, or eating at home.

For a half-liter of the excellent local beer (The Thirsty Monk, for example), you'll pay from $1 at happy hour to $2.50 in a nice place, with the average in the middle. In a store, the same size is 60¢ to $1. Good Czech beers sell for similar prices.

The wine in Slovakia is a pleasant surprise to many visitors, with the whites and dessert wines on par with what you'll find in Hungary: they share the Tokaj wine region. A good bottle of wine in a bar/restaurant averages $6 to $12. The house wine will often be $2.60 (two euros) or less a glass; sometimes much less. In a store, the majority of bottles are between $3.50 and $8, with only the premium brands hitting $10 to $20. There are some nice wine bars where you can sample a range of them without killing your credit card like you would at home.

The local firewater of choice is fruit brandy—usually made from plums, grapes, or pears—that's used as a digestive before the meal or as something drunk for hours until you're legless. A small glass in a restaurant or bar is 60¢ to $1.60 depending on quality, with a bottle of it starting at a few dollars in a store.

Coffee, water, and soda will all cost you more than a dollar at a restaurant or bar. It's economically unsound to be a non-drinker and shun the local tap water here.

Locals generally don't do much more than round up the bill for a tip, so 10% is considered generous.

Transportation:

Getting around is the big rub in Slovakia. The train system leaves a lot to be desired, for a start. Bratislava is connected to several other countries, but at the time of writing, from Košice you could go south to Budapest, but not north to Krakow. There's a connection from Košice to the High Tatras Mountains, but not to the capital. Where there is a regular connection, the express trains take no more than six hours and top out at a price of $24, some being half that.

The bus system is a better bet for most towns, once you make sure you're on the right one. A short 20 km trip will be around $2. The seven-hour trip from Bratislava to Košice is about the most expensive domestic ticket you can get, costing $23 or so. This isn't a real big country to get around.

City trams and buses are usually 70¢ for a short ride to $1.20 for something that will take an hour. It can be cheaper to get a one-day pass for $6 or so, or a multi-day pass for less per day.

Taxi fares are less than a dollar a km, but the flag drop can be two euros, so figure $5 and up for all but the shortest ride. Getting to the airport from the center will cost around $13 to $20 in Bratislava, $10 to $15 in Košice.

You can rent a bike for a half day for $5 to $6.

What else?

•   Slovakia is a great place to do winery tours and discover things you have never tried before, like Grüner Veltliner, Welsh Reisling, Furmint, and Lipovina. Several distinct wine regions produce soft reds, mineral-rich whites, and good dessert wine. Some of the wineries have inexpensive lodges or rooms for rent.

• There's an interesting area along the Slovakia/Poland border in the north where you can take a $10 or so wooden boat ride down the Danajec River bordering the two countries, through impressive rock canyons. There's camping and a few inexpensive lodges where it begins, plus this is a good area for hiking and cycling.

• There are only five million people in this whole country and not all that much industry, so it's easy to find a quiet spot in Slovakia. Hiking here really means getting away from it all.

• Small Slovakia doesn't have a whole lot of superlatives to boast about, but you can check out the "highest Gothic alter in the world" in the pretty town of Levoca.

• If you're into castles—or have kids who are—this is your destination. There are more than 100 of them scattered across the lands, from 13th century ones that held off the Tartars to grand manor houses with 20 bedrooms.

• This is a tough place to get online if you're not carrying your own device. Cyber cafes exist in Bratislava, but in a week I only saw one elsewhere.

• What you can get for a buck or less: a liter of milk, a kilo of potatoes, a small bottle of beer in a bar or restaurant, a glass of house wine, a shot of fruit brandy, a local bus or tram ride, admission to some churches and monasteries.

EUROPE

Bulgaria

In most respects, Bulgaria is the cheapest destination on the continent. Transportation for a pittance, bargain meals, and $1 glasses of wine allow you to travel well for cheap. Despite the bargains, there aren't many tourists here. You can visit major sites and be one of the few visitors there. Hiking in the wilderness in Bulgaria's many mountains really feels like hiking in the wilderness, not being part of a hut-to-hut pedestrian freeway.

The Bulgarians are a bit self-conscious about their state of affairs. They know they're at bargain basement level compared to the rest of Europe and aren't sure how to pull out of it. One journalist lamented in the national press that the country is defined by its cheapness, that tourists don't visit for the beautiful architecture, but "because we have the cheapest kebabs and prostitutes," plus "cheap beer and drugs."

I can't vouch for the hookers and drugs, but nearly everything else is indeed a deal here. There's one stumbling block: the language. It's a thorny one to figure out and the Cyrillic alphabet they use means you probably can't read any of the signs. I actually traveled with a tour company while I was there (see www.hiking-bulgaria.com) and was very thankful. Doing it independently in the countryside would have been tough.

If you could get everything for the Bulgarian price, it would be even cheaper. Accommodation prices are routinely inflated for foreigners, so unless you time it to arrive at the beginning or end of the tourist season, you'll routinely pay $6 to $12 per person on lodging. Another reason to go with a company booking everything in bulk.

An independent budget couple can do okay on $30 to $50 per day and a mid-range couple should be comfortable on $50 to $80, but it takes a bit of work to find good accommodation values.

Attractions include imposing castles, charming villages, intact historic city centers, and the beaches of the Black Sea coast. Nature is the best asset. Hiking is good in warm weather and there are places to stay along the trails. In the winter, you can also go skiing in the mountains, where an all-day lift ticket can be as little as $10. Historic and picturesque cities like Plovdiv and Veliko Turnovo would be thronged with tour buses if they were in Western Europe somewhere. Here you can almost have them to yourself.

Sofia may not rival Prague or Budapest for architecture and culture, but it's no slouch either. The Byzantines, Slavs, and Turks all made their mark here, and then the city really took off at the end of the 19th century and became more European. Sightseeing is interesting and the National Opera and Ballet Theatre offer cultural performances at bargain prices.

Under communism, Bulgaria used to be one of the world's most infuriating destinations. Endless bureaucracy, border hassles, maddening currency regulations, and only "official tourist hotel" choices kept foreigners (except Russians) at bay. Travelers still haven't come back in force, except for on the Black Sea coast, so the most parts of the country remain undiscovered gems.

Go outside of winter unless you're heading for the ski slopes. The off-season here is really off: outside of Sofia and the slopes, most hotel facilities are shuttered after September.

Accommodation:

Unlike in super-popular Prague or Budapest, there has not been a sudden surge of demand in Sofia to send lodging prices through the roof, but the flip side of that is there's not as much choice either.

You can generally camp in various places outside the capital for around $5 to $8 per person, but facilities can be rundown. Some campgrounds offer cabins or bungalows for not much more. Hostel beds cost more than they should but have actually come down in the past decade. They can be as little as $5 per person along hiking trails but are commonly $9 to $18 in the capital and in resort areas during the summer. Often this includes breakfast and Internet access, plus some will do bus station pickups and/or daily beach shuttles gratis.

Double rooms or suites in a private home (look for people at the train station or check the local tourism office) are sometimes the best bet at $5 to $20 per person—prices are much lower in smaller towns than in the cities. You can sleep in a monastery for $20 to $24 double and guesthouse rooms near a national park average a bargain $15 to $30 double. Unless you stay at an international 5-star chain, a deluxe hotel room should cost $50 to $100, complete with room service, minibar, TV, and a pool. The average licensed hotel listed room rate in the country was $83 a night in 2012. Obviously, you get more for your money as a mid-range traveler than a shoestring one. At the high end, anything going for more than $150 per night is rare. In many hotels, that will get you a suite.

If you want to spend some time at one of the Black Sea beaches, you may find the best deal is some kind of package tour booked from Sofia or even another European capital (to get a cheap flight). You'll pay less than if you tried to negotiate a rate on your own and will probably get meals thrown in as well. For better or worse, most of the beach crowds are there on a group charter tour. Don't expect much charm.

Food & Drink:

The biggest surprise for me when visiting Bulgaria was how great the food was and how massive the portions were. Even for an American used to supersized meals, I was amazed at how much food kept arriving. If you go between April and October, a lot of what you get will be very fresh and local as well.

Much of the food here is similar to Greek or Turkish cuisine, with lots of white cheese, bread, and yogurt offset by huge salads. (If you're a vegan, be advised the salads will also be covered with cheese.) In winter it can be more of a struggle for vegetarians: lots of meat dishes and hearty stews and soups. This is a real "slow food" country, so if you come in the summer, expect heaps of fresh fruits and vegetables. If you come in the winter, expect lots of pickled items on your plate. To me, the locals looked amazingly robust and healthy, so my visit really made me wonder about the supposed evils of eating too much dairy.

Eating on the street will only require a few coins: cheese-filled breads for 25¢, small pizzas for 50¢, or a sandwich and soda for $1.50 to $2.50.

Two- or three-course restaurant meals in a simple place will seldom run more than $5 to $8 each with drinks. If you spend much more than $10 each, it'll be a relatively atmospheric place or a tourist haunt; even in some pretty places with English menus, none of the main dishes will top $8. In general expect $2 to $6 for big main dishes and 50¢ to $1.50 for dessert.

The only time you'll spend a lot on food is if you try to satisfy a craving for something like Mexican or Italian food—your bill could hit $25 for two. Or you could spend more if you went to the nicest seafood restaurant at a Black Sea beach resort, where package vacationers are regularly in a free-spending mood. Tipping is not very common, but you'll be expected to round up the bill.

The beer here has gone up a bit in recent years, but is still probably the cheapest in Europe or darn close. Figure on 50¢ to 80¢ a liter in stores, $1 to $2.50 in a bar/restaurant for a liter depending on decor. A cheap bottle or poured liter of local wine will be $1 to $2.50 in a store or from a local and getting a good bottle of wine—in a country that has a lot of good wine—will often only cost you $10 in a restaurant. Locals sell homemade stuff by the gallon in smaller towns: pretty much every house has a grape trellis on their property somewhere.

The local firewater of choice is raki, but unlike the anise-flavored stuff of the same name in Turkey, here it's distilled from grapes or plums. It can be as little as 75¢ for a shot or in a mixed drink in a bar, but is usually a dollar or two. It's not uncommon to see a bottle of Russian vodka in a store for $2 to $3.

Herbal tea and water are the cheapest things to order to drink, with a step up from there being coffee for a dollar or so. This is another country where a soda is often more expensive than a beer or glass of wine. So act like a European and order something that goes better with food.

If you want to cook for yourself, you won't pay much. In the markets I saw at least 20 kinds of fruit and vegetables going for a euro a kilo or less.

Transportation:

With the local wage being around 120 euros a month, the government needs to keep transportation costs low. So getting around in Bulgaria won't put much of a hit on your budget; this may be the cheapest country to travel around in all of Europe. You can traverse the entire country (Sofia to Varna) by train for less than $15 and lots of shorter trips are $5. First-class is only 40% more, so it's an easy splurge. Buses can be faster and more comfortable, at a similar price of $3 to $12 on almost any route.

A taxi across town is generally 40¢ to 70¢ per kilometer. Getting from the airport to the center should cost less than $8. A 10-ride pass for the public buses, trams, and trolleys in the capital is only $4. You can rent a mountain bike in the smaller cities and in the countryside for $5 to $10 a day.

Long distance taxis are pretty affordable, especially in the rural areas. You can sometimes hire a car and driver for an all-day road trip or sightseeing circuit for $35 to $50. It's easier and cheaper than renting a car. Especially since you can't read the signs!

Most internal flights are under $60—this is not a very big country. You can often find budget European flights to nearby countries at low prices. A train from the capital to Bucharest, Romania is less than $25 and a sleeper berth to Istanbul from Veliko Turnovo is around $50.

What Else?
•   It is fairly easy now to get to Bulgaria by train (including from Istanbul direct to Veliko Turnovo) and budget airlines like Wizz Air serve the capital from many European cities for cheap.
•   There is an excellent network of hiking trails in the mountains, with free camping allowed along the way or the chance to stay in mountain huts and order meals. You may need a guide, if only to figure out the signs and maps.
•   Museums and attractions have been known to charge tourists five times what the locals pay, but at $4 or less for nearly any attraction in the country, it's hard to complain. One great bonus: monasteries are free.
•   Tickets for the National Opera and Ballet start at $4 and symphony tickets start at $3.50.
•   Bulgaria has some of the best ski prices in Europe, but on some very high and challenging mountains. Figure on $12 to $15 for equipment rentals, $20 to $38 for a walk-up, all-day lift ticket.
•   Haggling is not really common practice here, but complaining about inflated hotel or taxi costs will often result in a "correction." Souvenirs are cheap. Things to buy include folk art and ceramics, embroidered clothes, carpets, dolls, leather goods, communist memorabilia, and silver jewelry.
•   English is not widely spoken, especially outside of Sofia, and the local Cyrillic alphabet is tough to decipher. Carrying a decent phrase book at all times will make life much easier. Or

pony up a bit more and go with a tour company like Odysseia-
In (at http://www.hiking-bulgaria.com).
•   What you can get for a buck or less: a train ride to the next
town, a liter of beer, a bottle of cheap wine, a local bus/tram
ride, a short taxi ride, a kilo of vegetables, a liter of yoghurt, a
few street snacks, an hour of Internet access.

EUROPE

Hungary

Imagine visiting your local wine bar and ordering three different varieties from assorted regions, being served by someone who can explain the climate there and what awards that vintner has won. The chalkboard list behind the bar has over 100 wines by the glass to choose from and there's something for every taste. The interior is elegant and the location is perfect, right across from a busy pedestrian plaza fronting the city's huge historic cathedral. It's the kind of place you could linger for hours, but how much is it going to cost you when the bill comes?

$8.50 with tip.

That's what I spent at the best wine bar in Budapest. For three glasses that took my taste buds on a terrific ride, from three distinct wine regions of Hungary.

Hungary is a great place to start or end a trip through Eastern Europe. Many travelers who have been through Europe rate Hungary at or near the top of their list, or rank Budapest as their favorite city. The castles, beautiful baroque buildings, and people that have an unrestrained zest for life cast a charm. Tens of millions of people come here each year, but most only head to Budapest or to Lake Balaton.

For those willing to get into the countryside, the language can be a challenge, but it's one of the few places in central Europe where you can still get way off the beaten path. The architecture varies by area, with most being either medieval,

18th century baroque, or Ottoman in nature. The country is small enough to explore thoroughly if you have about a month but you could cover a lot of it in two weeks.

Wine lovers will have a heyday here: the winery tours and festivals are a great way to get familiar with the local styles and the prices are universally a bargain except for the most coveted vintages.

Hungary is known for its music and you'll find a wide variety of performances to check out.

With the rise of cross-border medical treatment happening in many places in the world, Hungary has jumped on the trend with both feet. Many Europeans come here to have dental work done or to receive good medical care at a discount.

Hungary joined the EU in 2004, but the country still uses the forint, which is a volatile currency. Prices in this book are based on 220 to the dollar, so check the current rate before cursing my name because prices have changed a lot. Most hotels are priced in dollars and tend to be a good deal at all budget levels, especially outside of summer.

A single budget traveler can get by on $30 to $40 per day here being frugal, and more than that will generally keep you well fed and in a nice bed, especially outside the capital. A backpacking couple should plan on at least $60 a day. Mid-range couples can travel very well for under $100 per day outside Budapest, but plan on at least $150 a day in the capital unless it's late autumn through early spring, when hotel rates drop.

July and August are high season here, packed with Europeans on holiday, retirees on river cruises, and students on their college break. January and February are tough times to visit: it's bitterly cold and many tourist attractions are shuttered.

Being a mid-range traveler here means you can afford to eat and drink almost anywhere a local would. Hungary ranks right behind Sweden as having the least income inequality in the world—there's not a huge difference between the top earners and the bottom earners.

Accommodation:

The big kicker in Hungary for backpackers used to be lodging, but prices have actually dropped since the first edition of this book came out because of greater competition. They're now 25% to 50% less at the low end than in Western European cities such as London, Amsterdam, or even Berlin. A hostel dorm bed will cost from $8 at the cheapest place in a small town, but generally $12 to $18 in the capital. Make reservations if you'll be here when the college students are all on break and you want to stay in a central area of Budapest. If you don't mind being further out, the university dorms are opened up to renters in summer and sometimes you can find one with two rooms and a kitchen for less than $20.

If you're carrying a tent and you're in Hungary between May and September, there are some 300 campgrounds scattered around. You'll pay a charge per person and per tent, generally a total of around $8 to $15 for two people with one tent.

Double rooms in a basic hotel or hostel range from $20 to $50 outside of the capital and you'll often pay the same price whether it's one person or two; find a friend if you're alone! The top of that range will often get you a private bath, TV, and fridge. (As a result, mid-range travelers may think the country is more of a bargain than low-end budget travelers will.) Full-blown deluxe hotels start at $60 in the countryside. The sweet spot of choice in Budapest is between $60 and $100 a night, where you'll often find 40 places or more to choose from, including 4-star chain hotels. Be sure to check Hotwire, because that's when you see the true bargains. Even when I checked mid-July prices there were 3-star hotels for under $35, 4-star ones for under $45, and one 5-star one listed for $67!

Homestays can often provide a good value, especially for singles, and you'll get a taste of how the locals live. People with rooms to rent will often be on the lookout for travelers at bus and train stations. In Budapest, you can line up a stay with one of the old ladies holding up pictures at the Keleti train station, they're not as common as they used to be.

In the wine country areas in Villany, and less crowded areas around Lake Balaton, there are some great guesthouses charging $16 to $30 a night double, clackety rental bikes, wine glasses, and a corkscrew included in the rates.

As in the Czech Republic, there are some unique hotels housed in castles and historic buildings, worthy of a splurge if it's in your budget.

Food & Drink:

You don't come to Eastern Europe to lose weight or become healthier. Heavy meat, cheese, and stew dishes predominate and anything that can be fried will be. Walk it off! Hungary is the home of paprika, however, so spicy stews, including goulash and fish stew, are popular dishes. There is a lot of variety on menus and you can afford to drink wine often here with your meal. If you're a carnivore with a bit of money to spend, you will eat very well. If you like salami and sausages, you'll be in heaven.

Vegetarians will get by with just a little effort in Budapest, but should do some research on other areas outside the capital and learn some local food language; otherwise you'll be eating nothing but fried cheese and mushroom stew. Apart from cabbage and peppers, there aren't a lot of fresh vegetables outside of summer and early fall. Most things are pickled. A meal without pickles here is like Budapest without the Danube.

You can eat street food for a buck or two and a full meal in a local joint will usually come in at $3.50 to $6. There are a million ways to spend more, and the rise of tourism in Hungary means that a lot of restaurants are now catering to those on a quick weekend trip or package tour. You can spend a fortune if you go for gourmet spots. Expect a 10% gratuity to be added to the bill and another 10% if there's live music.

There's a lot of good salami and cheese for picnicking. The pastries are one of the best deals you can find, with all kinds of goodies running 25¢ to a dollar, accompanied by an espresso or cappuccino for a buck or so more. Hungarians take their dessert very seriously! Some cakes and tarts are similar to what you would get in Vienna, but at one-fourth the price.

Alcoholic beverages are good and prices seem to have leveled off the past few years after rising for a while. The local beer has a long history of excellence and the wines, which were world-renowned before the commies ruined everything, are becoming more popular each year as the quality returns. The sweet Tokaji dessert wine is the most famous, but also try to get your hands on a bracing, mineral-rich white wine from the Balaton region, or a Cabernet Franc red from the Villany region. A local form of plum brandy is widely available in local restaurants and bars and offers the best route to a reduced bar tab—often a dollar a glass in the "ruin pubs" of Budapest.

You'll generally spend around a dollar for a beer in a store. Figure on $1.50 to $4 for a beer, glass of wine, or plum brandy in a restaurant. (But a glass of house wine is often about the same price as a Coke.) In the "Valley of the Beautiful Women" near Eger, a liter pitcher of local wine is usually around $2 to $3. Or just go from cellar to cellar doing tastings and buy a bottle or two of what you like direct from the producer.

You can find a decent bottle in a store for $2, something quite good for $4 to $8. If you spend over $10 you might end up with something from a "winemaker of the year" who has adorned local magazine covers.

Mineral water is expensive and often costs more than a real beverage at a restaurant. Go with tap water—it's perfectly drinkable and free.

Transportation:

The public transportation in Budapest is efficient and fairly easy to follow. It's expensive in relation to local wages: $1 to $1.50 per ride to get where you need to go in Budapest. A 24-hour subway pass for $6 is a better deal if you're on the move.

A minibus from the airport to your hotel will run about $6. Taxis are okay for a short hop, but at $2 to get in and $2 per km, the cost adds up fast. A cab to the airport runs $18 to $35 (more coming from the airport than going there).

The Budapest locals are bike-crazy and a lot of the main avenues have marked bike lanes. Some hotels and hostels have loaner bikes available, but you can also find rental kiosks with prices from $5 for four hours to $9 to $12 for 24 hours. Prices are generally lower in small towns but the quality may be iffier outside of Lake Balaton.

Inter-city buses and trains are relatively equal in price, but in some areas a bus is the only choice. Expect to pay a few dollars for a short hop or around $8 to $14 to go a few hours from Budapest to Eger or Pecs. The comfort level is good overall, especially compared to areas outside Europe.

For about the price of a rental car $50 to $75 a day), you can usually hire a car and driver for the day to get around the countryside. That way you don't have to decipher the road signs.

Train connections to the rest of Europe are plentiful and reasonable if you just get a seat. To Vienna is around $24, to Prague around $50. I took an overnight train to Transylvania in Romania and got a sleeper berth for $65.

What Else?

•   The Budapest Card from the tourism office can be worthwhile if you're doing a whirlwind tour of the capital, as it gives you unlimited public transportation and museum admissions for three days. At around $18 for 24 hours or $40 for 72, you have to really be on the move and it doesn't include the House of Terror museum.

•   Hungary is known for its historic spas and bathhouses. You generally pay a fee and have free reign to relax as long as you want. It's around $17 (depending on exchange rates) to soak at Hotel Gellert's spa. The Széchenyi is a vast 1913 complex of outdoor and indoor pools. For $15 you can laze around, watching the families frolic and the old men playing chess. Your admission to either allows you to hang out as long as you want.

•   Some of the major city museums have free admission to their permanent collections, including the National Gallery, and many famous sites are outdoors and free. Major museums are $6 to $9 in the capital, less in smaller cities.

•   When souvenir hunting in Budapest, try shopping away from the package bus crowds at the main tourist areas. Many prices are double in the Castle area and Vaci Utca. There are shops along the large streets in Pest that will charge much less for souvenirs. Bargaining is not really done in Hungary.

•   Be prepared to tip as much, or more, than you do in the U.S. Everyone who does anything for you will expect 10% and not giving a tip sends a signal that your service was poor. Make it a part of your budget.

•   What you can get for a buck or less: a cappuccino, two carry-out pastries, a short subway ride, a glass of cheap wine at a festival, a kilo of beets or potatoes, ¼ pound of dried fruit, a shot of plum brandy, a half-hour or more of Internet access.

EUROPE

Romania

The country of Romania hasn't yet seen the flood of new visitors experienced by Eastern European hotspots in Poland, the Czech Republic, and Hungary, but in the picturesque towns of Transylvania, you'll see plenty of other tourists—especially Germans. The country joined the European Union in 2007, but it still uses its own currency and feels many paces behind the European neighbors to the west, even Hungary.

There's not as much weekend getaway money floating around here as you see in Prague or Krakow, and Bucharest still hasn't been pronounced as "hot" by the glossy travel magazines. It probably never will be. There aren't a lot of luxury hotels there still and their former dictator destroyed a huge percentage of the historic buildings to construct his giant "palace of the people."

The main draws here are the medieval castles and historic churches in the Transylvania region—along with a dose of Count Dracula of course. This area also features a lot of unspoiled mountain scenery, good for hiking in the summer and inexpensive skiing in the winter. (Only Bulgaria has cheaper ski slopes.) The country has more than 400 parks and nature reserves.

There is the center of the Roma (gypsy) culture, with interesting music, apparel, and handicrafts. The Museum of the Romanian Peasant in Bucharest is one that has stuck in my memory long after a hundred others have faded away.

Bucharest will probably never make a list of the world's greatest cities, but it certainly has its charms. The historic houses that managed to survive communist rule are impressive and there are a lot of pretty neighborhoods jammed with fun pubs and restaurants, easily reached by the cheap subway. If you've got plenty of time, do a quickie tour and then head for greener pastures.

Overall, Romania is a good deal for backpackers, a fantastic deal for mid-range travelers on vacation. A backpacking couple could get by on $40 to $50 a day, but one spending $100 to $200 a day in Romania will really be living large. Keep in mind that Romania's currency fluctuates quite a bit, sometimes moving from 2.8 to the dollar to 3.5 (and maybe back again) within the space of a year. Hotels are often priced in dollars or euros, but anything else you spend money on is not.

Accommodation:

A place to lay your head won't hit you too hard here except maybe summer on the Black Sea coast. You can find a hostel bed as low as $5 in some spots, though $7 to $14 is now the average. As with Hungary, prices have actually gotten cheaper here since I first started covering the country because there's more competition. This has upped the quality level as well. Hostel and traveler hotel owners will usually throw in breakfast and a few freebies to give them a leg up: beer, filtered water, Internet access, a welcome shot of Romanian moonshine, or even cigarettes! The environment is competitive in most spots and you seldom need reservations outside July and August.

While much of the tourism industry in Romania seems to be filled with people who disdain tourists, the hostels are a different story overall: welcoming and well run. There are plenty of places to camp as well, which can be quite pleasant in the mountainous countryside. You'll spend more on transportation since they're outside of town.

Rooms are available in private homes for as little as $12 in the countryside, but $20 to $35 is more common. As more hotels have opened up, some of these options have faded into the background or have converted to proper B&Bs. You can get a room in some peaceful monasteries for under $20 double.

Mid-range hotels often have a bit of an institutional feel to them. Look for something in a historic building or something opened recently to better your odds. A 2-star room will run anywhere from $30 to $60, a 3-star room will usually come in under $70. The vast majority of hotels in Romania are under $100, even the international chain hotels like Hilton and Marriott. In the winter months you'll be hard-pressed to find anything priced higher than that, even in the capital. Unlike a decade ago, there's plenty of choice now in most locations.

The Black Sea Coast is the exception, with unimpressive hotels priced far higher than they should be. Expect to pay $50 and up for something tolerable in the summer, and more than $100 for a room you'll actually like. A package deal here can make a lot of sense. Or a better idea is just to avoid it altogether and save the beach time for some place nicer.

Food & Drink:

Romania is another country that doesn't pull in any visitors based on its food. You see lots of stuffed cabbage rolls, sausages, bland chicken and pork dishes, stews, salads made with mayonnaise, whole fish breaded and tossed in a pan, and soups seemingly made with whatever is lying around. It's tough eating Romanian and being a vegetarian, though it gets better in the summer when more fresh veggies are available.

You'll pay $3 to $5 for a budget meal, though it's easy to find cheaper options like pizza, kebabs, or street food snacks. Usually $5 to $15 will cover a meal in a nice restaurant and it's hard to spend much over $30 each anywhere without being a glutton. As in Turkey, you'll frequently be charged for extra items placed on your table in a restaurant—even butter. Wave away whatever you don't want.

On the plus side, many popular restaurants offer a lengthy menu and specials to lure you in are common. Set lunch menus with multiple courses are a good deal, and many spots have special deals for students and the elderly. Some will toss in a free glass of house wine.

The drinks are sometimes more interesting than the food. The beer is unheralded outside the country, but is quite good, generally $1.50 to $2.50 at a bar, much less in a store or at happy hour. Much of the wine is forgettable, but when a decent bottle is $3 to $5 at a store and not much more in a restaurant, it's hard to complain. Three are a few excellent wineries putting out good stuff if you seek it out. When I visited the excellent Halewood Winery, the most expensive bottle in their shop was $13—for sparkling wine made with the labor-intensive Champagne method.

In the countryside, a potent homebrew liquor called *palinca* is sold from plastic jugs for $3 a liter. *Tuica* plum brandy is touted as the signature local drink and is the cheapest way to get a buzz on if that's what you're after.

Transportation:

Getting to and around Romania is cheap. So cheap that some savvy travelers buy a charter flight package deal to a Black Sea resort, then throw away the second half of the ticket and go overland from there. Getting to Romania by bus and train is reasonable, but flight deals on cheapo airlines are common.

Within the country, trains are easier to figure out than the patchwork of competing bus companies and are a good value. A train ticket from the capital to Brasov, for example, runs around $10. A 100km train trip is generally $5 to $9. A bus from the capital to further north in the Transylvania region will come in under $15. The train network covers the whole country and is still quite popular. You can even take a train from Bucharest 14 hours to Budapest for around $75. I splurged $90 for a sleeper berth from Budapest to Sighisoara and ended up having the entire compartment to myself.

Local transportation is also a good deal, apart from the rip-off drivers greeting passengers at the airport. Try to arrange transportation with your hotel or a private company as what should be a $15 or so fare can balloon to $30 or $45 with these guys thanks to rigged meters. Or take the shuttle bus instead—it's $2 and is quite nice. Official taxis are a bargain, when they use the meter like they're supposed to, at less than 50¢ per kilometer. Local buses, trolleys, and trams are 40¢ to 70¢ per ride depending on whether you purchase a pass. You can get a 10-trip subway pass in the capital for less than $3.

Romanians have a well-deserved reputation as the worst drivers in Europe. Renting a car in Bucharest is about as much fun as being poked repeatedly with a pointy stick. It's slightly better in rural areas, but in most cases you're better off letting someone else take the wheel.

What Else?
• Looking for a place to ski for cheap? In the Transylvanian Alps of Romania, a day of skiing will run you $20 to $45 (lift tickets are on a point system determined by which lifts and how many rides you take). Ski rentals are around $15 a day.
• At least a million Romanians have moved abroad to work since 2007 and the funk in Europe has hit real estate developers hard. If you're looking for a cheap vacation home or ski chalet, poke around here. One developer in the resort area of Sinaia was giving a free car with condo purchase when I was there.
• Want to walk in the steps of Vlad the Impaler, who inspired the story of Count Dracula? Head to his birthplace and have an overpriced dinner in the house where he lived as a boy, then see Bran Castle where he was imprisoned for about $8 .
• You can do multi-day hikes through the Carpathian Mountains, staying at strategically placed cabanas for $3 to $12 per night.
• Music performances are often $2 to $10 depending on seating. They sell for half-price the day of the show.
• Museums and attractions won't break the budget here: most are $2 to $4 and very few dare to charge more than $6— the most notable exception being the King's Peleş Castle

outside Sinaia, where you could drop close to $50 if you took both guided tours.

• What you can get for a buck or less: a happy hour beer, a cheap glass of wine, a shot or two of plum brandy, six liters of bottled water, 100 grams of olives or white cheese, a slice of pizza, at least a half-hour of Internet access, student price admission to most museums, two subway rides, a short taxi ride, a grilled kebab, three sesame bread *covrigs* (*simits* in Turkey) a town-to-town local bus ride in Transylvania.

EUROPE

Europe - Honorable Mention

Czech Republic Outside Prague

Prague is arguably the best-preserved city on the continent, full of some of the finest Baroque, Art Nouveau, and Cubist buildings in Europe. Unfortunately, it also represents one of the most stunning tourism explosions in history, in many ways becoming too popular for its own good. Hotel prices in the capital have increased so quickly that the city is almost on par with the cities of Western Europe. The mobs pouring out of bus tours turn the city into a sort of gothic Disneyland in the summer. This is the Czech Republic that some 90% of the country's visitors see.

Outside the capital, however, it's easy to get away and find a more relaxed and inexpensive atmosphere (except in the historic spa towns). Outdoor enthusiasts will find plenty of hiking opportunities; you can enjoy spectacular views and caving around Moravian Karst, and bargain ski resorts are open in the winter. At least a dozen major chateaux and castles are a day trip away from the capital, and you can find folk festivals and local wineries in the Moravia region.

This is perhaps the best country for biking in all of Europe. There's a really well marked and maintained system of trails covering much of the country and extending across borders to Austria, Slovakia, and Poland.

The small medieval city of Cesky Krumlov is a highlight for many travelers, and Jindrichuv Hradec will work even better for beauty without the crowds.

The Czech Republic's costs vary greatly depending on exchange rates. When it's around 20 to the dollar, life is good, at 16, not so much.

As in Budapest, lodging is an expense that's out of proportion to other costs in Prague. If you can find a reasonable hostel bed, you can travel fairly well here for $25 to $40 per day at the budget end as a single. Couples can get by on $40 to $70 a day as backpackers, or $70 to $130 per day at the mid-range level.

Your chance of being on the lower end of this range increases as you spend more time outside of Prague. You can easily pay $300 a night there, but in many towns the best inn around may be $60 for a double. A few castle hotels can be a worthwhile splurge.

In Prague and some other tourist spots you'll often run into a two-tiered pricing system. Be especially diligent at nice-looking restaurants or you're sure to get taken for a tidy sum.

Food and transportation are a good deal here, so if you are staying with friends, the country can be as cheap as many others in this book. Getting from the second-largest city of Brno to Prague runs less than $10 on a train or nice bus.

The best value of all is beer, glorious beer! The Czech area is one of the world's great historic beer producers and Pilsner originated here. It's uniformly excellent and it flows freely and cheaply. Expect to pay around 80¢ to $1.40 in a local bar for a half-liter, up to $2 in a nicer restaurant. This, for a beer that makes the new world version of "Budvieser" taste like nothing more than yellow fizzy water.

Turkey

The country of Turkey was always on the verge of getting pulled from this book due to rising prices and this time they had to get downgraded for sure. I would highly recommend a visit to this fascinating country for anyone armed with an ample vacation budget, but as per capita income for Turks has doubled in the decade since the first edition of this book debuted, prices have gotten out of the range of backpacker travel.

There are a few reasons for the increased prices, and for Turks they're all good ones. The country has gotten steadily more popular each year, often growing the number of visitors by double-digit percentages. More tour companies have trips there, more cruise ships are stopping, more flights are going into Istanbul, and there's more positive press on traveling there each month. Most of the 25 million+ people who visit come back raving about it. In addition, the Turkish economy has been humming along nicely, in stark contrast to what's going on elsewhere in Europe.

For a vacationing mid-range couple, this is all well and good, as standards and infrastructure have improved. Hotels in this range haven't gone up all that much and restaurants are still reasonable by European standards. Sightseeing will hit you hard, which is part of the reason Turkey is now a tough place for backpackers. Visiting nearly any major historical site will cost you $9 to $20, so if you try to see most of what's worth seeing in Istanbul, you could blow a week's backpacker budget in a day or two.

It's now nearly impossible for a couple to get by on less than $60 a day in western Turkey unless you can do your own cooking at the guesthouse, or have people to stay with now and then. But $80 to $100 a day enables a reasonably comfortable shoestring lifestyle if you're not moving around too much. A single person can do okay traveling alone here ($50 a day bare minimum, more in the summer) since there are a fair number of hostels with dorm rooms and small single rooms in the pensions. Sightseeing admission charges will bust the budget in a hurry, so Turkey is not a place to get by on the bare minimum. (Also, beer prices have crept up as the conservative government has held onto power.)

In the middle range, the main difference is accommodation, as transportation and food are a pretty good deal everywhere. Expect $120 to $250 a day for two people to have a nice hotel room with TV and maid service plus three good (but not lavish) restaurant meals per day, seeing the sights regularly.

If you head east, standards take a dive and the population is more conservative, but the prices are certainly cheaper. The divide between tourist zones and regular Turkey is pretty huge, much as it is in Mexico.

Some sites are worth it, others are a downright rip-off, so study up on what you want to see and ask around for other travelers' impressions. Prices are usually more reasonable in the countryside, but parts of Cappadocia will ding you for an admission charge.

The Turkish hospitality is legendary and if you subtract the carpet dealers and touts in Istanbul, you'll probably find the Turkish people to be some of the most honest people in the world: the only place I've felt safer is in Japan. Turkey is also one of the easiest countries for a woman to travel in alone. You'll be seated next to other women on buses, led to a "family room" or area in some restaurants, and you'll seldom be harassed by men on the street.

Turkey is a great tourist destination and I'll be heading back there a few months after this book is released on a writing assignment. I'm sure I'll have a blast. But if money is tight, the other European countries highlighted here will enable you to stretch your money further.

THE AMERICAS

For residents of the U.S. and Canada, Latin America is a natural first choice for adventurous travelers. You can get to any capital in Central and South America in a few hours or on an easy overnight flight, and you seldom deal with jet lag from major time zone changes. In general, the flight prices are lower than those to Asia or Europe—especially when you factor in fuel surcharges, which many airlines serving this region don't add on. There's not much anti-American or anti-Western sentiment (well, outside Venezuela anyway), and it's certainly not hard to find ways to learn some Spanish. That one language will carry you from Mexico down to the bottom of Argentina. It won't help you in Brazil, but that country is way too expensive for this book anyway.

While none of the countries in Latin America are quite as cheap as the bottom rung in Asia, you won't need a lot of dough in Guatemala, Honduras, Nicaragua, Bolivia, or Ecuador. Plus if your flight was half the price of one to there, that can make up for it if you're just going for a few weeks. If you've got the time, you can also cover it all overland—Mexico to Patagonia—except for a boat between Panama and Colombia.

Mid-range travelers will find all of these countries to be a terrific value and they'll be happier than the shoestring travelers with their accommodation: the best values are often revamped colonial homes in the $35 to $75 range.

There's a whole different vibe here than you'll find in other parts of the world, with distinct music, dancing, food, and traditions. You seldom feel like you are anywhere close to home.

"Different" means scary to some people and the chaos and noise can be overwhelming sometimes. When it comes to real crime however, in much of Latin America you're safer than you are at home, no matter what Fox News says. There are exceptions where you need to exercise special caution. Venezuela has become a dysfunctional state with high crime—

part of the reason it's not in this book. Honduras is in this book and it's as bad or worse there as I write this. Both countries are over the 60 murders per 100,000 mark. Honduras, and to a lesser extent Guatemala, are key smuggling routes for drugs heading north. Stay away from the crossfire by avoiding the Moskito Coast and capital of the former, and Guatemala City of the latter. And of course, steer clear of the Mexican border towns if you can.

Transportation is cheap throughout the region. It won't always be comfortable, but you can see a lot of different places without killing your budget. The trains usually aren't much help, so you'll spend a lot of time on buses. The good thing is, the nice buses are really nice for the price. There's a well-defined "Gringo Trail" in this part of the world, so you can often find a very comfortable bus for just a few dollars more than the cramped one that stops every 100 meters. Internal flight prices are seldom a great bargain, but are reasonable outside of Argentina and Peru. Honorable mention Mexico now has a fully competitive selection of airlines on many routes.

As in other chapters, I've left out some notable countries in the region. Costa Rica is popular for its rainforests and eco-tourism, but costs continue to increase each year as the country tries to bring in more wealthy travelers. With the number of U.S. and Canadian retirees numbering in the six figures, being a budget traveler there can be trying, especially when it's time for dinner or an adventure tour. This is a place where booking an air and hotel package deal can make a lot more sense than going independently. El Salvador and Paraguay are certainly cheap, but there aren't a lot of compelling reasons to visit. Brazil and Chile can cost you as much as you would spend at home.

I have left out cheap but belligerent (and increasingly dangerous) Venezuela from the honorable mentions: I'd rather send travelers to places where they are wanted. I have kept Mexico there, however. I go to Mexico every year, just lived there for a year, and own property. I think it's still a great value if you do it right, but the Mexico that most visitors see is not where the deals are. You have to work a little harder and get out of the beach resort areas. If you do it right, Mexico is a great value.

After having Argentina in this book for a decade, I've dropped it this time. While the Argentine peso is at 4.6 to the dollar as I write this—up from 3 to the dollar in the first edition—inflation has more than eaten away at those gains. Hotel rates have roughly doubled once you get outside the hostel range, plus the food and transportation costs keep going up. Adding insult to injury, Argentina has joined several other countries in adding a mandatory reciprocal visa fee that will cost you a bundle of money upon arrival at the airport. For Americans, it's around $140 per person. Plus currency restrictions and other protectionist measures create ongoing headaches for travelers. (ATM withdrawals are limited to around $80 per day, for example.) See more in the Honorable Mentions section.

Latin America is a huge area geographically, so it is hard to make many generalizations. When it comes to meals, however, especially lunch, you can find an inexpensive set meal in nearly any town between Tijuana and Tierra del Fuego. Except in progressive cities such as Buenos Aires and Mexico City, and in resort areas, bars are mostly a male affair. Machismo rules throughout Latin America, so women traveling alone need to have thick skin (or good enough Spanish to hurl insults back). Apart from the Mexican border towns and some pass-through routes in Central America where the drug cartels are sponsoring shootouts, however, the whole region in general seems to get a bit safer each year and tourist crime is increasingly rare. If you look at the stats, your odds of getting shot are certainly far worse in the average U.S. city.

Brush up on your Spanish though. This is one big patch of the globe that is in no real hurry to learn English. After all, a Chilean man from Patagonia could travel all the way up South America, through Central America, to the tip of the Yucatan without speaking anything but Spanish—as long as he avoids Brazil. He could then hop on a boat and visit Cuba, Puerto Rico, and the Dominican Republic and travel or do business some more without uttering a word of English. So while the people who deal with tourists all day will speak English in Latin America, learning a bit of Spanish will make things much easier, especially if you intend to travel on a low budget or to get off the beaten path.

THE AMERICAS

Guatemala

Nearly everyone who goes to Guatemala now has positive things to say about it and there's no denying that this country the size of Ohio packs a lot of attractions into an inexpensive package. It's also easy to get to: it shares borders with Mexico, El Salvador, Honduras, and Belize, and flights from the U.S. and Canada are relatively short.

Unfortunately, that location makes it an automatic pipeline for the overland transport of drugs. Guatemala actually has a much higher murder rate than Mexico, with the added frustration that most of them don't get solved. This is a country where you definitely don't want to mess with the wrong people. Fortunately, most of the wrong people are in Guatemala City, which is best avoided anyway because it's not very attractive.

With nearly half the population being of Maya descent, rather than European, it feels more like a foreign culture here than, say, Argentina. Many people come just to visit some of the numerous Maya ruins and monuments, including the granddaddy of them all at Tikal.

It doesn't stop there, however. The colonial city of Antigua is one of the region's most enchanting destinations, offering plenty of creature comforts as well. Most travelers also spend some time kicking back in one of the villages surrounding Lake Atitlán (surrounded by mountains and three volcanoes) or seeing the huge Maya market in the highlands of Chichicastenango. The adventurous can hike in rain forests, climb around live volcanoes, or go white-water rafting on raging rivers.

The scenic trip down the Río Dulce from Lake Izabal, through the gorges, to the Caribbean coast area of Livingston, is also worthwhile. The Caribbean coast region is far different from the interior, with a laid-back beach scene of good dancing music, coconut bread, and fresh fish. The west coast has just so-so beaches, but there are a few surf spots and good fishing options.

Some backpackers come here and end up staying far longer than they'd planned. Call it the spell of the mountains or a lulling sense of relaxation that's hard to shake, but sanctuaries such as Finca Ixobel (in the Petén region) and the largest towns on Lake Atitlan are brimming with people who forgot to leave.

Guatemala is a popular destination for immersion courses in Spanish, with a Latin American slant that's more useful to those who want to use it in this hemisphere. (Many Spanish courses and tapes are based on European Spanish, rather than what has evolved in this part of the world). Courses can be arranged through universities for credit, or directly with the language school for those just wishing to advance their communication skills. It's a bargain if you do it direct. My wife, daughter, and I had 20 hours of private lessons each over a week and paid a shade over $400—including the homestay with a local family. Prices have stayed at this level the six years since then.

Guatemala can be a great place for shopping. The signature colorful weavings are made into everything from clothing to purses, but there is also a great selection of bead jewelry, leather goods, sweaters, blankets, and rugs.

A hard-core backpacker could still get by on $15 to $20 per day here—especially if staying pretty stationary in the countryside—and a couple could travel fairly easily on $30 to $50 per day by taking chicken buses, eating where locals eat, and limiting the time in the main cities. Prices haven't really gone up much since the first edition of this book came out a decade ago, partly because tourism has stayed relatively flat.

By spending $60 to $100 per day, a couple could consistently stay in comfortable hotels, eat good restaurant meals, and travel on shuttle vans, seeing everything they want to see. Spending more than this puts you solidly in the mid-range level, with lots of escorted tours, taxis, and nicer hotels in each town. Costs vary a lot by area, with the ones attracting vacationers (Antigua and Flores/Tikal especially) commanding higher rates on nearly everything. If your itinerary only includes these types of towns, Guatemala will be more expensive than less-touristed Nicaragua and Honduras. There are plenty of short-term package tourists and students in Antigua, and near Tikal, so things are priced for free-spending travelers.

If you're the type that cares about the impact of your tourism dollars, you could do a lot of good going to Guatemala. The massive mudslides and floods that hit after Hurricane Stan in late 2005 barely made the news, but they devastated a large swath of the countryside near Lake Atitlán, causing some 700 to 1,000 deaths, and destroying around 35,000 homes. Smaller earthquakes since have wiped out whole villages. The Maya people are still struggling more than they should be overall, with most of the country's wealth going to a relatively small slice of the population.

In general, very few tourists encounter violence in Guatemala, but travelers still need to keep their wits about them and employ common sense. It is better to travel during the day except when long journeys are necessary, and the usual pickpocket precautions apply in Guatemala City. A late night of staggering through Antigua drunk and alone will probably not end well. Though it's hard to believe, there's even a law against pot in some areas from the copious amounts in use, getting caught with drugs can involve a nasty sentence in a nasty jail. If indulging, use common sense, be respectful, and be discreet.

Accommodation:

As one guidebook so accurately put it, "From every crack in Antigua's cobblestones sprouts a budget hotel." Wherever backpackers and other travelers congregate, you'll never be at a loss for lodging.

At the budget level, you can generally find a basic double room with shared bath for $7 to $10, or $8 to $20 with a private bath. Singles and dorm beds range anywhere from $2.50 for a dark cell (or an especially great find), to $10 for one with a hot shower and sheets. The best deals are in the off-season, or in spots where there is plenty of backpacker competition. Residents in some towns offer home stays for around $50 per week, when they're not all set aside for Spanish language course students. There are plenty of long-term rental options around Lake Atitlán for a couple hundred dollars a month.

For a step up, mid-range travelers will find plenty to choose from in the popular tourist areas. If there's enough competition, you can get a nice double room with a hot shower, maid service, and cable TV for $20 to $35, so you don't have to spend much more to get a bump up in quality. In most areas, $40 to $60 will get you a suite that sleeps 3 or 4 people and has a pool outside. There are more than a few expensive adventure tours that come through Guatemala, so there are also hotels that are relatively luxurious, usually topping out at $85 per night for the best room you can find outside of Antigua, Flores/Tikal, and the capital. Meals are sometimes included as you head up in price. There are only about a dozen hotels in the whole country charging more than $120 per night for a standard room.

In all tourist areas, prices tend to be a bit higher in July and August. The weather is not ideal then, but it's when more North Americans are on vacation and more college students are taking Spanish classes.

Food & Drink:

As in much of Central America, expect to eat lots of corn tortillas, rice, beans, eggs, and chicken. There is little food distinctive enough to set the region apart from its neighbors. The tourist influence in Antiqua has raised the bar much higher and you can find all kinds of inventive dishes there. Dishes with avocados and *mole* sauce are a nice treat here and there, and the coastal areas feature lots of fish, seafood, and coconut. Bakeries offer some substantial snack options, including inexpensive sausage and cheese rolls. Soursop is a popular fruit and joins many others at bargain-priced juice stands.

You can generally find a big breakfast or lunch set meal plate of local fare for $2.50 to $4 almost anywhere you find lots of local workers chowing down. International food and a nice atmosphere will raise the meal price to the $5 to $20 level in tourist areas. It's pretty difficult to spend more than $20 on a full meal with drinks anywhere unless you order wine, which must be imported. Street food snacks and fruit are available for cheap.

There are so many gringos in the country's popular tourist haunts that you won't have any trouble finding vegetarian food or good desserts. Unlike many other Latin American countries where all the good coffee gets exported, you can find a quality cup in restaurants and cafés in any sizable town.

The local beers—such as Gallo, Moza, and Dorado—are mostly routine lagers, but are easy to find and there is one malty dark beer version. At a dollar or two, they can double the price of your meal. Wine is rare, but rum is not. Expect to pay as little as $3.50 for a bottle of cheap rum to $20 or so for some of the best stuff in the world—Ron Zacapa Centenario, aged 15 or 23 years. A rum and Coke is often the cheapest drink around.

Transportation:

Roads in Guatemala are not exactly akin to motoring on the Autobahn. For most travelers, there's no question about springing for at least one flight within the country, especially the one from Antigua to Flores (near Tikal), for $50 to $90 each way.

City to city transportation is no picnic here. There are very few bus lines offering "luxury" bus trips outside the most popular routes. The local buses are cheap, but are merely converted school buses on their second life—often after living out their usefulness hauling U.S. school children. Combined with some rough mountain roads, it can be trying. But at least they're cheap: expect to pay a buck to get from Guatemala City to Antiqua, or less than $14 for the 13-hour trip from Guatemala City to Belize.

A better bet for those not on a bare-bones budget is to join up with or directly hire a private tourist shuttle. A seat on one of these will be worth the premium. It'll cost about $8 to get from Antigua to Lake Atitlán, for instance, then $12 to $14 to go the other direction. Overland buses to neighboring countries can take a while, but they're easy to find. Tourist companies run some routes regularly, including from Flores (near Tikal) to Belize and Mexico. You can get an express bus from Antigua to Copán, Honduras for around $15.

Thankfully, apart from Guatemala City, you can walk everywhere you need to go in the towns, including Antigua. In Guatemala City, you may pay up to $5 for a cab across town, but if you're spending much more than that you've been ripped off. The buses cost pocket change if you can figure out the route and squeeze on.

A ferryboat ride across Lake Atitlán will run $2 to $4 depending on distance.

Car rentals don't make much sense in Guatemala. You're better off hiring a driver for the day. Getting a van full of people from the Flores airport to the entrance of Tikal, or from Antigua to the Guatemala City airport, is generally $30 to $60.

What Else?

•   You can take a tour of a local coffee plantation from several tourist spots, including Antigua and Cobán, and see the origins of your morning jolt.

•   You'll pay 10 times what the locals do for museum admissions, but most are still $4 or less.

•   You'll find ATMs and places to cash traveler's checks in cities and tourist centers, but take along enough cash to go for days in rural areas, including Tikal.

•   If you're a beach lover, head to neighboring Belize or Honduras (there's a boat connection to the Honduran Bay Islands from Livingston). The small strip of coastline here pales in comparison.

•   If getting a scuba certification in the ocean freaks you out a bit, you can get PADI certified while diving in a lake at Santa Cruz—for less than $275.

•   Several companies offer white-water rafting excursions and it's possible to get on a trip at almost any time of the year here. In Antigua you can rent a bike for about $1.50 an hour, or go on a half-day guided bike tour for about $20.

•   Guatemala leads the region in the proliferation of Internet cafés and some coffee shops have Wi-Fi. You'll have no problem staying in touch.

•   What you can get for a buck or less: 15 to 20 bananas, a local breakfast, a rum & Coke in a bar, two great cups of coffee, 15 rolls, two pounds of potatoes or tomatoes, at least a half-hour of Internet access, four local bus rides, a short tuk-tuk ride, 10 miniature Maya dolls.

THE AMERICAS

Honduras

Honduras offers a wealth of geographic beauty, including some stunning island beaches that are postcard perfect. The Bay Islands offer some of the cheapest scuba courses in the world and some diving packages throw in a free (or close to it) hotel room in the off-season. All this, in spite of having the second longest reef in the world right off the shore.

Adventurous travelers can also find plenty of hiking, white-water rafting, and sea kayaking options. The country also boasts the impressive Maya ruins at Copán, as well as some dense jungles full of wildlife.

There's just one catch: thanks to drug runners having their way with a coast and river system that's hard to defend, this is now the most dangerous country in the Americas, if not the world. News reports say a local is 80 times more likely to be murdered than one in Europe. It probably doesn't help that guns are "limited to only five firearms per person." So far few tourists have been affected, but forget the talk about Mexico—this is where the narcos are *really* in control. If you're an inexperienced traveler who gets spooked easily, you're probably wise to steer clear of Honduras for now. If not, at least avoid the two main cities and be very wary about touring the Moskito Coast. It's a jungle out there in more ways than one.

The U.S. government has stepped in with equipment and training to help, so this could eventually turn around like it did in Colombia, but keep an eye on the news before landing.

Honduras, the original "banana republic," is a poor country, right behind Haiti and Nicaragua. This is the second-largest country in Central America, but much of it is undeveloped or set aside as barely managed nature reserves. This means that there are plenty of bargains, but the most developed tourist facilities are in a rather narrow range of locations—namely Copán, Tela, La Ceiba/Pico Bonito, and the Bay Islands—with the islands putting forth a far more luxurious face than the interior. Even if you stick to these spots, you'll find Honduras to be a great value. Venture further afield on a local bus and you can sleep and eat for very cheap.

The West End of Roatan Island is known as Gringo Central. It's the most expensive area in the country, but this is a relative term and many weary travelers think they've arrived in paradise when they see the spotless rooms, international food, and great bars. Rooms are $10 on up to $200 here—the latter all-inclusive—and gourmet meals can hit $20 per person, but both are of a high standard and some of the beaches here rate up there with the best in the world. So unlike in the popular areas of Belize, what's above the water is as attractive as what is under the water.

In the rest of the country, prices have barely budged since the first edition of this book was released: the local lempira currency declined to a level of 19 to the dollar in 2004, stayed there for years, and then crept up to 20. For those who come from EU countries, it's even more of a deal. Currency aside, prices are just very inviting in Honduras. The most expensive hotel in Gracias, for example, is under $40 a night for a double. Drink piña coladas 'til you're legless and you'll be out $10 or $15.

Travelers who wish they'd been born in the age of explorers can see what it was like by going to one of the huge protected rainforests and cloud forests, almost completely populated by indigenous locals. Village guides are generally $8 to $15 per day depending on group size, and most of the transportation is via foot and canoe. A tent, a water purifier, and plenty of food supplies and insect repellent are necessary once you leave the village. Most visitors end up seeing plenty of wildlife, including tropical birds, monkeys, crocodiles, and a variety of butterflies. The jaguars that haven't been poached keep to themselves.

The town of Copán Ruinas, near the great archeological site, is one of the nicest towns you could ever chill out in. Nearby Santa Rosa de Copán is a center for growing coffee and making cigars. You can see the process for both in action: tour a coffee plantation and see a "factory" where quality hand-rolled cigars are made.

Do some climate research before you go unless you're just planning to visit the islands. Temperatures and rainfall can vary drastically according to location and altitude.

In general, the crime here has gotten worse since the last edition of this book and by any means necessary, avoid the capital city of Tegucigalpa. There's no "must-see" anything here anyway and drug gangs are a serious problem. The larger the town/city, the more precautions you should take, especially after dark. This is especially not a good country for single women to stroll around late at night, swinging their purse.

Backpackers can coast on $15 to $20 per day fairly easily here, depending on their comfort level and how much they're on the move. As usual, couples sharing rooms will spend less per person. When I was in Honduras last, I met several couples easily sticking to a budget of $20 to $30 a day. Mid-range couples can be fairly comfortable on $40 to $80 a day unless staying in Roatan during high season or taking advantage of the diving packages. If most of your time will be on an island, double the budget. If you're diving, triple it. Even at bargain rates, scuba diving is an expensive sport.

Accommodation:
Budget travelers can find a dorm bed or basic single room for as little as $2 in many areas. Most dorm beds and singles range from $3 to $8. A basic double with shared bath is $3 to $10, anywhere from $5 to $15 with a private bath. The upper

end of the range usually includes hot water and the occasional satellite TV. Long-term rentals are available in a lot of areas for $100 to $300 a month.

There are very few top-end hotels outside of the islands and big cities. You can generally find a nice mid-range hotel for $20 to $30. From $20 on up, you'll usually get air-conditioning and often a pool as well. If the equivalent of a three- or four-star hotel is available, it'll be anywhere from $30 to $90 in most areas, though in Roatan you can spend several times that if you're looking for first-class.

On Roatan and Utila, book ahead or be prepared to shuttle around looking for a place to stay: despite a building boom and a struggling tourism sector, the better places get filled up fast when the islands are busy. For travelers of any budget range, a dive package here (rooms, meals, and diving) is the best value anywhere in the Caribbean.

Food & Drink:

Expect the staples of tortillas, beans, rice, eggs, and potatoes, with plenty of seafood anywhere near the coast (including lobster dishes for well under $10). A fish soup with coconut milk is a standard dish, as is a similar concoction with vegetables served over rice. The yucca vegetable finds its way into a lot of dishes here, and there are Honduran versions of burritos.

You'll also find plenty of burgers, pizza, and kebabs. There are fast food options for the homesick in the cities and plenty of international choices in tourist spots. Vegetarians won't have much of a problem in the tourist centers, especially on the islands. The influx of expatriates in the Bay Islands has given birth to a huge variety of international cuisines there, with good bread and dessert to boot.

Breakfast is usually a tortillas/eggs/beans concoction, with some fruit here and there, often for less than $1.50. Other meals range from a dollar for a quick burger or burrito to $6 for a three- or four-course meal or pizza at a local eatery. A set meal in a basic local joint is often around $2. The most

159

expensive main dish I found in the whole town of Copán Ruinas was $12—at the best hotel in the center.

A beer in a restaurant or bar will average a dollar or two depending on how fancy the place is, with the price dropping below a buck during the numerous happy hours. Salva Vida is the most popular, but some others similar lagers pop up here and there. Rum is a good alternative for those on a budget and fruity cocktails are commonly $2 or so on the coast.

Transportation:

There is an extensive bus system and it's easy to find a connection from one point to another. Finding a comfortable one can be another story, however. You can sometimes find an "executive" bus that costs double the normal fare. Since this only amounts to, say, $2 instead of $1.25, it's well worth it. In general, the regular buses run about 80¢ to $1.50 an hour. A city taxi ride will rarely top $5 (not metered) and local buses are usually less than 20¢.

Internal flights are quite inexpensive ($30 to $100) and can be a reasonable splurge to avoid a long bus trip or ferry ride.

The boat trip out to the Bay Islands is $16 to $20 and a flight isn't a whole lot more. Island hopping boats run regular trips or you can hitch a ride with someone making a supply run.

You can easily cross to Honduras from Guatemala by land, with Copán being a short hop from the border. A nice bus or van shuttle from Copán to Antigua, Guatemala runs $12 to $20. There are also land crossings to Nicaragua and El Salvador, as well as boat and land connections to Belize. Check a current guidebook for all the options and prices.

Honduras is only a two-hour flight from Houston or Miami and direct flights to Roatan are available from those airports as well as Atlanta and New York.

What Else?

•   Honduras used to be the cheapest place in the world to get certified as a scuba diver and though prices have risen to allow better safety measures and equipment, it's still not bad. Figure on $249 to $279 for a four– or five-day open water PADI course. If you're already certified, it will be $20 to $25 per dive, with volume discounts available.

•   If you don't want to dive down to caves and shipwrecks, many sites are accessible to snorkelers. Bring along your own set or rent it for $5 to $8 per day.

•   When you're ready for a different culture here, just head to the coast. Trujillo and other coastal cities are much more Caribbean, with lots of seafood, great music, and all-night dancing.

•   There are many spots in the Americas where you can do canopy zip-lining through the jungle, suspended by a wire. But here this is no Costa Rica extravaganza for the big money crowd. Costs are as low as $20, including transportation to the site (which may be on a horse...).

•   Lots of places offer a one-hour massage for $8 to $15.

•   Rafting the Cangrejal River in Pico Bonito National Park is a unique experience, the rafts flying around boulders as big as a house. At $35 to $40 including transportation and your room for the night, it's a steal!

•   Things to buy: woven baskets, woodcrafts, musical instruments, cigars, coffee, and ceramic items. Don't buy anything that's slightly heavy unless you can carry it out or send from another country. Shipping costs are out of hand.

•   What you can get for a buck or less: breakfast, a burger, a beer, a hand-rolled cigar, two or three cups of coffee, three sliced pineapples or huge mangoes, a fruit shake, two coconuts with a straw, a kilo of oranges, a small wood carving, a half-hour or more of Internet access, admission to some museums, more bananas than you can carry a long distance.

THE AMERICAS

Nicaragua

Costa Rica without the crowds, a frontier that's hard to find anymore, and a place where you can backpack around for weeks and spend just a few hundred bucks - that's Nicaragua. Don't come to enjoy ruins from ancient civilizations or go sightseeing in the traditional sense. Come to take pleasure in the great, unspoiled outdoors and explore a land where there are few signs of mass tourism.

It was unthinkable to include Nicaragua in the first edition of this book in 2002 because the infrastructure was just too basic and almost nobody was talking about going there, much less actually doing it. A few years later it was suddenly the hot destination. The government aggressively wooed foreign tourism investment and put a lot of money and effort into improving the road system and the wireless network. Forward-looking investors started opening up inns and restaurants at a rapid pace, especially in the colonial city of Granada and in the beach area around San Juan del Sur.

The road forward has been as bumpy as some of the back roads, primarily because of the fears of the country's ex-Sandinista leader following in the steps of Hugo Chavez and becoming a leader for life. The fear seems to be subsiding as I write this, and the Nicas worry less than we do because they are seeing clear progress at every income level. There are still huge problems in this poor country, but life is getting better each year for the average family.

The travel media has fallen in and out of love with Nicaragua several times now, with the lack of luxury hotels being the main reason the momentum has not kept building in the glossy magazines. There are now several comprehensive guidebooks to the country and even a *Living Abroad in Nicaragua* guide published by Moon. As a result, tourism keeps growing by double-digit percentages each year and new businesses are popping up each month to meet demand. It doesn't really matter whether the chicken or the egg came first; the organic growth is impressive.

A decade ago it took a very intrepid traveler to enjoy what Nicaragua had to offer. It's getting easier now each year to find a nice place to sleep and eat and find a way to get around.

This is still a long way from being Costa Rica or even Guatemala when it comes to development, however. The country is still quite cheap for a reason: don't expect a lot of five-star hotels, air-conditioned, express buses in every town, or gourmet restaurants. Expect all that Costa Rica has to offer, though, in a natural sense—and then some. Huge lakes with islands, perfect volcanoes, pristine jungles, and stunning beaches you can have all to yourself. If you've ever fantasized about strolling down an empty beach for miles without seeing another person, you can still do it here. In some spots you won't even see a house or a boat.

If you're one of those travelers who gets frustrated with throngs of tourists being around all the time and you like to go exploring where few have gone before, this is your place, especially in the northern regions and down the Rio San Juan. Traveling around Nicaragua won't always be comfortable and you'll sweat a lot, but if you can live with that, you can feel like a real adventurer, with a blank slate in front of you. There are no great ruins or monuments that draw throngs of vacationers, so the package tour crowds mostly give it a pass. As guidebook author Joshua Berman says, "Getting off the beaten path is as simple as hopping a rainbow-colored bus to a town whose name you can't pronounce."

The historic colonial town of Granada is an exception to the no-gringos rule; it gets a large portion of the country's visitors, and for good reason. The interesting architecture and spectacular setting on a lake facing a volcano gives it the air of a less-touristed Antigua (for now). After roaming around the countryside, the well-run inns, good restaurants, and bustling bars will come as a welcome break.

Nicaragua is one of the best deals in the Americas for backpackers. A single traveler could scrape by on as little as $10 to $15 a day here staying in the cheapest dorm beds and eating like a local, but that takes some work. A budget of $20 per day single, $25 to $50 for a couple is easier to manage. As always, it depends on where you are and how long you stay put. Accommodations in some areas here take a bigger chunk of the budget than they do in other cheap Central American countries. There just aren't as many traveler lodges in a lot of spots for the backpacker crowd, so often you really get what you paid for—or less—at the very cheapest places. Food is a bargain, and the typical converted school bus from place to place won't cost much. Most of the attractions are of the natural outdoor kind, so figure guides and local tours into the budget here and there, but next to nothing for city sightseeing. At the beach, most of your money will go toward beer (or rum) and food.

Mid-range travelers can do better since the majority of hotels in populated areas fall into this range. A couple could stay, eat, and adventure somewhere in relative comfort for $60 to $100 a day, though remember that comfort may fly out the bus window when it's time to move on. Since tourist facilities are still in their infancy, you can't blow a whole lot more than $150 a day as a couple outside Managua and Granada unless you're searching out the best hotel and restaurant in each town and taking a lot of organized day trip tours. Outside of these two cities and select beach resorts, only a smattering of hotels charge more than $80 a night double and spending more than $20 each on dinner is nearly impossible outside Managua and the two main tourist towns.

Organized tours booked locally are commonly $8 to $30 per day per person for something that returns to your hotel, or $40 to $80 for an overnight trip with lodging and a meal or two. "Hop-on, hop-off" tours on a set route are usually around $10 per person.

Be very wary about skirting the law here. Nicaragua has one of the worst legal reputations in the world for its corrupted justice system. On the plus side, the drug runners haven't gotten much traction here, and the murder rate is lower than in Costa Rica or Panama, one-fifth that of Honduras.

If you're looking to live on the cheap, this is a good place to put down roots. Many retired couples coast on less than $1,000 a month, despite having a maid and eating out a lot. Spend double that here and you're living like royalty. There are also attractive incentives in place for retirees.

Accommodation:

Cheap hotels in Nicaragua are a mixed bag and can often be less than safe or desirable. When you have a choice of cheapies, prices can be amazing. At the very low end, expect to pay $3 to $8 per person for a dorm bed or the most basic rooms with shared bath, except in Granada and Ometepe, where both choices and standards are higher. Outside the cities, some places will let you pitch a tent or string up a hammock for $2 to $3. In any town where there's some backpacker traffic, there will be plenty of choices for basic double rooms in the $6 to $20 range. For this price, you won't usually get hot water or air-conditioning in the high season, but I got the latter and a private bath for $7 on Ometepe Island while researching this edition. Don't automatically discount a place without hot water: when the tank is black plastic on the roof, the shower water is usually at least lukewarm during the day.

In the $25 to $60 range, you'll often get cable TV, air-conditioning, a fridge, and maybe a swimming pool or bar. (Don't pop into an "auto-motel" by mistake: these are love hotels rented by the hour.)

Lots of hotels include breakfast in the rates, plus the backpacker places will often throw in an hour or more of Internet access as well on their computers. Wi-Fi is usually free and more places have it than not. It may not be all that fast though: often it's from a mobile carrier rather than a wired cable or DSL line.

Upping the budget results in more choices and generally good quality—if you're not too far off the beaten path. In most towns and cities there are not a lot of fancy boutique hotels, but Granada is an exception. There you can now find a few dozen places, mostly run by westerners or elite Grenadians that combine friendly service and nice amenities for around $50 to $140 double, usually including breakfast. If you want to really splash out, there are a few resorts like Morgan's Rock and Aqua Wellness Resort, near San Juan del Sur and Jicaro Island Lodge near Granada, where you can spend a few hundred dollars a night. There are still only a handful of these in the whole country through.

A few villa rental options are starting to pop up here and there, with foreign property owners renting out their home while they are away. Most of these are in Granada or on the Pacific coast. If you want to stay in one place for a while and have a family or need a kitchen, these can be just the ticket. You'll see houses for rent advertised in Granada also; from humble local affairs for $200 a month to restored mansions for that much per night.

Food & Drink:

At market stalls or basic lunch counter places (*comedores*), two or three dollars will cover a hearty set meal with several items and a hibiscus drink. Fried rice and beans is a common working lunch and there are a lot of plantains and tortillas. Some kind of meat, often chicken, will be on offer but watch out for the locally popular tripe (*mondongo*)! *Fritanga* barbeque places supply a heap of meat for a few dollars. Vegetarians may not have much variety in larger towns without going for foreign food, but in rural areas, where there is less money, there will be far less meat and it is no problem. Overall, the food is seldom fancy, but portion sizes are more than ample. All-you-can eat buffets are often $4 to $8.

If you're a conscious eater, it's easy to find organic, fair trade, sustainable fare in Granada and the higher-end hotels. As soon as farmers here figured out they could charge more by just putting aside the pesticides and returning to manure and compost, they went all-in.

The hippest restaurant in any place besides Managua, Granada, or San Juan del Sur will usually result in a tab of less than $15 per person, including several courses and a beer or two. Granada has seen much of the recent investment boom, so hip new eateries catering to the *Condé Nast Travel* crowd are available in restored colonial mansions. Compared to what you would pay at home, even these are a bargain.

Bodies of water are always nearby, so a whole fish for dinner will often be only two or three dollars.
Nicaragua's rum is good and the Flor de Caña brand is on every convenience store shelf. It's a great bargain here, with the 7-year version available in a bar for under $5 a half-liter—glasses, ice, limes and cola included. A large bottle of it is about $7 in the supermarkets, with the 4-year being $10 a half-gallon. Get the cheap stuff instead and you can get legless for two bucks. A normal-sized beer will run 60¢ to $1 in a bar, or $1.50 to $2 for a liter-sized bottle. Figure on half that in a store or at happy hour. All but one are basic light lagers that all taste about the same, but in this heat they're a welcome sight.

Some of the discos in León charge a $5 cover charge, but then it's open bar for a few hours. In some dance clubs, the norm is to buy a bottle to split between friends, the set-ups and mixers included.

Transportation:

The regular buses in Nicaragua are mostly converted school buses well past their glory days, discarded by U.S school systems and on their second life here. At least try to get on an express *(expreso)* bus when possible, since in theory they won't stop at every little station along the way or pick up people waving alongside a road. These will only cost about 60¢

to 80¢ per hour, so getting from place to place isn't going to cost you much more than soreness and a gallon of sweat.

When there's an express minibus available, do anything you can to snag a seat on it if your budget allows. At a premium of only about one-third more than the jammed express bus, it's well worth the extra cents, especially since it will also shave time off the trip. A regular slow bus from León to Managua, for instance, can take two-and-a-half hours and will cost about a dollar. A minibus will take an hour-and-a-half tops and will cost about $2.50. The one from Managua to Granada was $1 as this book went to press.

Unless you are on an organized tour, a tourist shuttle, or have arranged a top-end car and driver, don't expect air conditioning. Tourist door-to-door shuttle vans are comparatively pricey ($20 to $40 for Granada to San Juan del Sur, for example, depending on group size), but can be worthwhile if you're in a hurry or have a group that can charter the whole thing at a negotiated rate. Plenty of them compete for the routes between Granada, Managua, León, and San Juan del Sur. They can especially be worth the premium to go straight to the Managua airport from Granada, avoiding the need for a taxi at the other end. Or when you arrive at the airport and want to skip the capital. Assume $30 to $40 between Granada and Managua if you're alone, but the more people you have in your group the less it will be per person.

Local buses aren't worth the hassle in the capital unless you are with someone who knows the routes. If you manage, they're a few cents to ride. In other towns and cities, the bus system is simpler (and less frequented by pickpockets.) Taxis start at less than 50¢ in most cities and it seldom costs more than a couple of dollars to get across town. In Managua, rates start at around a dollar and top out at about $6. The taxi from the Ometepe ferry dock in San Jorge to the bus station in Rivas is $1.50 or less (depending on your bargaining skills.)

Hitchhiking is accepted practice, especially in the rural areas. At times, it is the only way to get from where the bus drops you off to where you need to go. Offer something to the driver at the end of the ride, though much of the time it will be refused.

Boat transportation is required in some areas and with these often being quite remote, it can cost one to three dollars per hour on a long trip. The ferry from San Jorge to the main port on Ometepe is $1.50 to $3 depending on whether it's small and open or large and air-conditioned. Ferries across Lake Nicaragua, on the other hand, are a bargain (when they are running). A first-class, air-conditioned seat on the overnight trip from Granada to San Miguelito is less than $9. (Second-class is $4, but can get crazy crowded.) Schedules can be erratic with wind, waves, and bad business practices all contributing to uncertainty, especially March through May.

Renting a car here is as expensive as it would be at home, but the danger factor is twice as high. For the same amount of money or less, you can usually hire a car and driver, and then have someone who actually knows where he is going. You are also less likely to be pulled over by police, with a fabricated excuse to give you a ticket.

In the main tourist centers, it's easy to find a bike for rent ($3 to $8 per day), or a scooter/motorcycle ($12 to $40 per day). Kayaks are often a few dollars an hour at lakeside places. For all, prices vary by quality, demand, season, and your bargaining patience.

Internal flights are available for some routes and can be well worth it for long distances. Prices keep rising but are still reasonable in international terms: around $100 for a round-trip flight from Managua to the Corn Islands for instance, or $120 round trip to San Carlos from Managua.

You can take a long-distance bus to the nearest large city in Costa Rica, Guatemala, El Salvador, or Honduras for $10 to $35 depending on your departure point. If you're a glutton for punishment, you can ride all the way to Mexico.

What Else?

• The town of Masaya, about 40 minutes from Granada, is the country's handicraft center. It's easy to get here on a day trip and pretty much everything on offer anywhere in the country is going to be in at least one of the stalls here. Take time inspecting the quality and bargain patiently.

• Near Masaya are a few lake beaches: in Nicaragua you can lay on a beach on a lake, by the Pacific, or on the Caribbean Sea of the eastern coast. Just don't expect world-class resorts except a few around San Juan del Sur, which is also the place to arrange surfing, sailing, or fishing trips.

• The Corn Islands, in the Caribbean Sea, would be paradise if it weren't for the lack of infrastructure and the islands' strategic advantage as a drug-smuggling stop. It is painless to visit it for a weekend though; tour companies offer round-trip packages from Managua for around $400 including flights, two nights hotel, meals, transfers, and "all the rum you can drink."

• The island of Ometepe is the fresh-water island with the highest altitude in the world. Two volcanoes—one active, one not—rise up to over 4,000 and 5,000 feet. The small towns here are a great base for hiking through virgin forest and then kicking back with panoramic vistas. Parakeets and monkeys outnumber the residents. All but the most experienced backcountry travelers should hire a guide when climbing Nicaragua's many volcanoes; numerous cases of lost, injured, and dead tourists will attest to this.

• Almost nobody needs a visa for Nicaragua and you get an automatic three months upon entry. Take your time...

• If you're a baseball fan, you'll have no problem indulging your passion here. Unlike most Latin American countries, where soccer is a national obsession, baseball is the most popular sport by far in Nicaragua.

• As in most of Central America, dental care costs here are a fraction of the cost up north. Figure on less than $50 for a cleaning and check-up, $200 for a crown, $400 for a bridge or root canal.

• What to buy: hammocks are the top choice, but other handicrafts include ceramics, embroidered blouses, woodcarvings, items made from coconut shells, woven carpets, and leather goods. (And a bottle of fine rum makes a nice gift.) Fine cigars are big too, but watch out for "Cubans" which are

170

usually Nicaraguan fakes, albeit made of tobacco grown from real Cuban seed.

• You can work out your muscle tensions for cheap here: a massage at Healing Hands in Granada, for example, is $10 for 30 minutes, $15 for an hour.

• What you can get for a buck or less: a short taxi ride, an hour or more of Internet access, admission to the best museum in the country, a full lunch at a simple market stall, a one-hour or less express bus trip, a good cigar, a liter or two of bottled water, a liter of milk, two pounds of seasonal fruit, a fruit smoothie, a 25-minute phone call to the U.S., a pint of cheap rum, a happy hour beer in a bar, two cups of good coffee, 200 grams of cashews, admission to the bell tower in a Granada church, a haircut, or a stuffed toad.

THE AMERICAS

Bolivia

Bolivia

Bolivia is, on most counts, the least expensive country in South America. It also offers a wealth of beauty: dramatic Andean peaks, high altitude Lake Titicaca, the largest salt flat in the world, vibrant local cultures, volcanoes, jungle wildlife, and colonial architecture. Despite the bargains, however, this is a destination that has not yet caught on with a whole lot of tourists. In part, this is because its government has traditionally been always on the verge of collapse or a coup. Protests routinely shut down highways, and border agents will go on strike just for the heck of it. Plus the reciprocal visa fee (what your government charges Bolivians, they charge you) means a high price of entry before you even leave the airport for some nationalities. As an American, I had to lay out $135 in crisp U.S. dollars upon arrival.

Things are more stable now in the government, but the Chavez-aligned president hasn't made many friends in the U.S. or Europe and there's almost no promotion of the country by the government or the private sector.

Most travelers here are either backpackers making their way south or north, nature enthusiasts, or hardcore mountain climbers taking on some of the most daunting peaks outside the Himalayas. A few companies offer overland trips from Uyuni to the Atacama Desert of Chile, which I can say from experience is one of the world's great journeys.

The national parks here are short of facilities, but that means a wealth of unspoiled wildlife for those willing to make the effort. An organized tour across the bizarre salt plain landscapes of Salar de Uyuni is $25 to $75 per day well spent. Pick your guide company carefully, however. There are around 90 tour operators in Uyuni and at least a third are estimated to be fronts for laundering cocaine smuggling money. One traveler summed up the experience aptly when he said, "Our driver had 'I don't give a f#&* stamped on his forehead."

This is a country where indigenous tribes make up half the population and you'll see a wide variety of traditional dress on parade. Much like the hill tribe areas of northern Laos and Vietnam, people here are dressing up to please themselves, not tourists. This even includes the men. During festivals, you'll find the population in full regalia and the atmosphere will be intoxicating. (So will the gallons of homemade booze.) This is a land of quintessential South American postcard photos: a woman in traditional dress leading a llama, with snow-capped Andean peaks in the background.

Keep an eye on the news if you are planning a trip to Bolivia. Whenever the population gets annoyed with the country's leadership, which is often, blockades and demonstrations shut down the transportation system. It seldom turns too ugly, but more than a few travelers have gotten stuck staying a few days to a week longer than they expected.

A single traveler can get by on $12 to $25 per day here and a backpacking couple can do okay on $25 to $40 per day. Of the three main expenses, accommodation is the dearest, but there are bargains to be found in that area as well. Mid-range couples will be pretty comfortable on $40 to $80, depending on itinerary and hotel choices. A couple spending more than $100 a day will be living large.

Accommodation:
The few hostels that are in Bolivia average $3 to $6 for a bed. You can generally find a hotel room with shared bath for

$3 to $6 per person. A decent double room with bath will start around $7 for two in a cheaper city and up to $15 at a more expensive location. I paid $8.50 a night in Sucre at the end of 2012 and had a really nice room with private hot water bath, breakfast, and Wi-Fi.

It's a pretty big leap up to the three-star level. I paid $32 in Potosi for a more standard hotel in the center and wished I had my old Sucre room back. A room with TV, maid service, etc. will start at around $25 and can reach $65 in some spots. Expect everything to be a bit rough around the edges, or to be more frank, poorly maintained. There are only about five hotels in the whole country that could charitably be called "luxury." Many times the top properties outside La Paz are filled up by tour groups, so book ahead. In some locations the top spot will list for $120 a night, the second-best hotel will be $75 a night, and everything else will be $60 or less.

Food & Drink:

Bolivia's food is better than most people expect, especially for carnivores, though if you're coming from Chile or Peru, you'll likely feel like you've taken a step down. In general, expect lots of meat and rice, with some shredded lettuce or fried potatoes being the vegetable accompaniment. You'll often find a bottle of hot sauce to spice things up and some of the dishes can be scorching. Beef and chorizo sausages usually show up in one form or another, though in rural areas you'll find more vegetarian dishes.

The *menu del dia*, or fixed lunch, will keep you filled up. It generally consists of a starter or salad, large bowl of hearty soup, a main course with sides, dessert, and possibly coffee. These *almuerzos* generally cost fewer than three bucks and you can sometimes find them for as little as 75¢. This is the main meal for many Bolivians, so dinner is not as large. Filled meat or vegetable pastries (*empanadas* or other names) are a popular snack that you can fill up on cheaply while on the go for 50¢ to 75¢.

It's not hard to find a quick snack on the cheap in Bolivia. Two bolivianos seems to be the standard price for a bag of popcorn, a packet of peanuts, some dried beans, or even a basic ice cream cone. That's around 30¢ U.S.

There are a few good local lagers and several malty dark beers that show up here and there. If you're invited to drink with some locals, you'll be downing either *singani* liquor made from grapes (similar to pisco) or some maize liquor that's one step up from moonshine. A beer is sometimes less than a dollar in restaurants and seldom tops $3 for a liter. The most popular local wine costs $2 to $4 a bottle and Chilean wine is about 1/3 less than you see it for at home. Drink up here if you're heading to Chile because beer and cocktail prices triple when you cross the border. Watch the altitude: take it easy for a few days, especially if you're coming from sea level. La Paz is the highest capital in the world.

You can find juice stands everywhere, offering all kinds of flavors. About 35¢ to 50¢ will get you a glass full. *Api* is a spiced, non-alcoholic drink made from corn and is often sold with inexpensive sweet pastries. The coffee is good and strong and a cup of ubiquitous coca tea helps the altitude sickness.

Transportation:

Transport inside Bolivian cities is cheap and surprisingly efficient, though pollution from the old buses with no emissions regulations is an issue inside or out. Taxi rides in central La Paz should cost a dollar or less. In a smaller city like Sucre, Potosi, or Uyuni, the only trip that should cost more than a dollar is to an airport or outside of town. Shared taxis cost around 70¢ to 85¢ for longer distances and buses just a few coins. Minibuses fill in the cracks to everywhere else.

The railway system is pretty useless in general, but there are a couple of trips worth taking for the scenery, including one from Uyuni to Calama in Chile.

Buses will get you everywhere for cheap, generally a few dollars for a trip from city to city. Upgrading is a no-brainer if the schedule works. The regular bus from Sucre to La Paz, for example, is $10, but the "semicama" better one is $13, and the executive one that has three seats across that lean way back is less than $20. The splurge is even easier to justify for shorter trips, like $2.50 regular from Sucre to Potosi, $5 for the best bus possible. Note that the cheaper ones run far more often though, and are comfortable enough for short trips, with assigned seats.

Internal flights are inexpensive and reliable. You can get from the capital to almost anywhere for $100 or less. I flew one-way from La Paz to Sucre for $72 in late 2012 and had two airlines to choose from.

What Else?
• If you'd like to put down roots for a while, you won't have to spend much to do it. Some adventurous expats rent apartments in the capital for $200 a month. It's less than that elsewhere. Visa restrictions don't make it easy to stay long-term.
• Stores and markets are full of beautiful wool and alpaca sweaters available for $5 to $15. (Yes, the ones you've seen in shops at home for $50 and up). You can also find some beautifully made musical instruments, including panpipes and something resembling a ukulele. If you like strange hats, you'll find some winners to pick from. Many of the items that are popular in Peru are on sale here too—for far less money.
• If visiting during the high season (June to September), get an idea of when and where the local festivals take place. Otherwise you could land in town to find the rooms all booked.
• Bolivia's one ski resort offers the highest ski run in the world. Don't expect much in the way of equipment.
• You can see a movie for less than $3 and many cinemas have a 2-for-1 night on a certain weeknight.
• Bolivia is a budding location for Spanish language immersion opportunities, offering a more adventurous alternative to Mexico, Costa Rica, Ecuador, or Guatemala.
• What you can get for a buck or less: a few day's supply of coca leaves, two hours of Internet service, a trip to the local

bath house, a kilo of clean laundry, a 10-minute phone call home, two empanadas, a few Bolivian chocolates, a pair of wool gloves, snacks for three from a street stall, a kilo of rice, ten bread rolls, two liters of bottled water, a box of teabags, a kilo of seasonal vegetables or fruit, a few rounds of pool, a cab ride to the bus station, 10 eggs, a basic set lunch, a fortune telling session.

THE AMERICAS

Peru

Let me start this chapter off by saying Peru continues to get more expensive each year, especially for visitors who spend most of their time around Cusco and hiking the Inca Trail. However, Peru often pops up as the favorite of travelers who have spent a lot of time in South America. The scenery really is as spectacular as any glossy travel magazine spread and the prices are low enough to allow the average tourist to do and see everything. And "everything" is a lot here: desert canyons, mountain cities, the Amazon rain forest, Andean peaks, and of course those Inca ruins. Peru is the home of Machu Picchu, the continent's most popular tourist attraction, but still arguably one of the most magical sites on Earth.

It is the allure of Machu Picchu that is most to blame for the price increases, though a strengthening local currency hasn't helped either. Peru's tourism visitor numbers are going up at an annual rate of 10% to 15% each year, but Machu Picchu is already at or past sustainable capacity and the Inca Trail departures are booked up months in advance. So the price increases are partly a way to keep growth in check and partly a way to fund sustainable tourism initiatives and conservation. (Plus, the cynical will say, a way for leaders in Lima to make foreigners fund more of the national government budget.)

Good intentions or not, those on a backpacker budget will find themselves laying out a lot of cash to hit the highlights. Regular admission to Machu Picchu has gone from $20 to $45 in one decade (plus $6 for the bus ride up to the ruins), and you have to reserve tickets in advance. The train ticket out through the valley from Cusco starts at $48 one-way. A good Inca Trail tour has now passed $500 for four days—almost three times what I paid in 2005—with about a quarter of that going to fees and taxes. A tour in the Amazon jungle region can cost even more. A mandatory multi-attraction ticket for Cusco and the Sacred Valley is $48 ($26 with an ISIC card), whether you hit every attraction or not. Then there are the temptations of all the adventure tours on offer everywhere. There's a lot to do and see here, so you'd have to forgo a lot of worthwhile options to get by on a shoestring budget.

In all fairness, many of these high prices are for a good reason. The Inca trail used to be literally trashed, maintenance was lousy, and the porters were badly exploited. As prices and regulations have both increased, the trails, monuments, and people are all better off. But now you've gotta pay to play.

The central hub for most travelers is Cusco (or Cuzco), a stunning city perched at over 11,000 feet/3,500 meters above sea level. From here, travelers can set out for Machu Picchu or many other Inca ruins in the Sacred Valley or just wile away the days in a beautiful, historic Andean city.

The colonial city of Arequipa is another highlight, with white-capped mountains in the background of the main plaza and a rambling monastery that is a photographer's delight. Travelers with more time can tour nearby Colca Canyon, see the mysterious Nazca desert drawings, take a boat trip on Lake Titicaca, or visit the "poor man's Galapagos" of Ballestas Islands near Paracas, and that's just the south. There's plenty more to see and do off this main tourist route in the rest of the country and more interesting ruins up north.

Some of the finest trekking in South America is in Peru, especially around the area near Haurez, in the northern half of the country. The massive mountains reach to 18,000 feet and are permanently topped with snow.

Almost ten percent of the country is in some kind of protected zone, be it national park, national forest, or sanctuary of some kind. Some of these are as large as a small country. The Manu National Park and Biosphere Reserve and a few others boast some of the greatest diversity of flora and fauna on the planet.

Peru also sits in the middle of a popular budget traveler's circuit of Ecuador, Peru, and Bolivia. It's fairly simple to go to all three countries overland and alternatively, many travelers go to Bolivia as a side trip from Peru: Lake Titicaca straddles the two nations.

Accommodation:

Prices in Peru are quite reasonable outside Lima, where the cheap hotels start at $18 per night double but most are $30 and up. Many of the low-end ones in the sprawling city tend to be pretty undesirable, so it's worth spending a little more to get a room that's clean and in a safe area. Since Lima is usually only a one or two-night stay anyway, it's worth it to splurge.

In the popular travelers' town of Cusco, the launching point for Machu Picchu, budget dorm beds are available for as little as $6 in the low season, though $8 to $14 is more the norm. Double rooms at the bottom end are $12 to $40 depending on quality, seasonality, and whether you are sharing a bath. The best places in Cusco fill up quickly in May through September, so it makes sense to book ahead there. The upper end of that range will sometimes put you in a restored colonial mansion with a courtyard, or a room with a stunning balcony view. Mid-range travelers can easily find a very nice hotel with plenty of amenities for $45 to $80 double, including breakfast. Of course Machu Picchu is a prime tour destination for those $6,000 and up "adventure tours" you see advertised in glossy travel magazines, so you can pay plenty more around Cusco if you want—or $800 a night for the hotel right next to the ruins in Machu Picchu.

Outside of Cusco and Lima, hotel prices are generally lower, with some of the best rooms in town routinely on offer for $70 a night. All bets are off in the jungle. Most of the jungle lodges are booked as part of a package tour, as a circuit or short excursion from Cusco, so hotel prices are lumped into the total. Choices range from bare-bones huts with six-legged pets to fancy digs that will make you forget there are a hundred wild critters outside your door.

Food & Drink:

Peruvian food seems to have gone from completely unknown to "hot cuisine" since the first edition of this book came out and generally the hype is well-placed if you're dining in a nice restaurant. Some local dishes are not for the squeamish, as in roasted guinea pig, bull penis soup (yes, really), and another soup made with boiled cow hooves. Get away from the sensationalist TV show fare, however, and the food is quite impressive overall, especially at nice restaurants on the coast and in the capital.

More standard fare includes pastries stuffed with meat, a wide variety of potatoes, corn, rice, chicken, plenty of fruit, and lots of seafood, especially ceviche. The food varies widely from region to region, however, and you'll actually have an easier time finding pizza these days than you will finding a roasted guinea pig. For most travelers, the food ends up being a pleasant surprise. At the cheap places it's not amazing, but it's consistently good and filling, and a nice break from the beans/tortillas/rice diet of much of the Americas. Quinoa is actually the most popular grain in the Andes region and is used in a lot of dishes. You can eat healthy here without trying too hard.

The street food is cheap and filling, with kebabs, fried potatoes and sausage, and empanadas being the most common. You can always get a cheap meal at local markets, or stock up for a hike or picnic. Mild cheeses and sausages that can be sliced like salami are easy to find. In the cities, there are plenty of cheap set meal places and local fast food options outside the tourist areas. Spit-roasted chicken restaurants are also numerous.

In the mountains, expect plenty of vegetables and rice, with a bit of meat thrown in for flavor. In the jungle, bananas, plantains, yucca, rice, and river fish are the staples. Along the coast, you'll find plenty of ocean fish and scallops, though the preference for ceviche preparation (not cooked, but cured in citrus juice) probably isn't a wise bet for just-arrived western stomachs. Wait a few days.

You can generally find a set meal in a locals' restaurant for $1.50 to $4, or $3.50 to $9 in a tourist restaurant. This will include a soup, main dish, bread, and tea or coffee. The dining scene is so competitive in Cusco that even the smallest tourist restaurant will usually throw in a free glass of wine or pisco sour to get you in the door. Chinese food is available in most towns and there are ample vegetarian choices in the cities and tourist areas.

Going up a notch, spending $8 to $14 per person on a meal will enable you to eat almost anywhere, with pretty surroundings, maybe a fireplace, and cloth napkins. There are only a handful of restaurants outside Lima where a couple would spend over $70 on dinner, almost none outside of the five-star hotels. You'll be expected to leave some change for a tip if a service charge isn't included. If there's a music performance, you'll find an additional charge tacked on and fancier places also levy a hefty tax.

Fruit juices, bottled water, and sodas (including "Inca Cola") are everywhere. Novel alcoholic beverages include a kind of beer made from cassava and another homemade version fermented from corn, plus some local firewater that will leave your head throbbing the next day. Peruvian wine is a hit and miss affair, but it's seldom more than $8 a bottle in the stores and $3 a glass at a restaurant. Better stuff from Argentina and Chile isn't much more. Most beers are similar regional lagers that are good enough, but you can also find a malty black beer here and there. They run from $1.25 a bottle at happy hour to $1.50 or $2.50 other times. Peru is proud of its pisco and this clear grape brandy is sipped straight or mixed in cocktails. It'll sneak up on you, especially at high altitudes.

Coca tea is not only legal, but encouraged. It provides stamina on your treks and helps with altitude adjustment, without giving you any real buzz: think coffee without the shakes or the comedown afterwards.

Transportation:

Peru is ten times the size of England, with close to 30 million people. This is not a compact country to travel through: it can easily take 12 hours to get from one place to the next on a bus, or 20 hours from Cusco to Lima across the mountains. And then there are the altitude changes. It's best to take your time, pick one area to explore, or spring for some overpriced internal flights.

Most locals travel by bus, which means you can always find a ride to where you're going. They're cheap as well, with a trip from one end of Peru to the other costing $35 in the lowest class. There are ample choices here in terms of comfort and the Pan American Highway is in good shape in the flat areas. Figure on $1.25 to $3 per hour of travel for a good bus and even less for the converted school buses serving mountain routes. At the top end, you'll have comfy reclining seats, heat/air-conditioning, and video entertainment (like it or not). At the bottom you'll ride with anything that can fit through bus doors. Rates come in at $22 to $50 for a bus from Cusco to Puno, $38 to $60 for the long trip from Cusco to Lima.

In contrast to most countries in Latin America, there are a few nice train trips worth taking in Peru. The thrice-weekly trip from Cusco to Puno, for example, is slower by train, but the scenery is better. Spring for an upper class seat and you'll have waitress service and fine dining. The train trip from Cusco to Machu Picchu also offers Andean vistas along the way, whether you take the backpacker class or spend $590 (round trip, with meals and Machu Picchu admission) to ride in the opulent cars of the Hiram Bingham express, run by the Orient-Express Company.

There's a duopoly on flights here (LAN and TACA) and you'll pay more as a foreigner than locals do, so they cost far more than they should considering the durations. But, a flight can chop a few days off the itinerary for travelers with a limited time frame. A round-trip flight of Lima to Cusco routinely runs over $400. You'll get hit with a hefty departure tax of close to $31 when leaving the country and each airport levies a tax for domestic flights.

Renting a car comes with the usual road hazards and expenses here ($45+ per day), but can really free up the schedule if you have a group of people striking out to see the countryside. Hiring a car and driver can work out even better for the Sacred Valley area since he'll know where he's going. Expect to pay $65-$85 for a day with a Spanish-speaking driver in a taxi, more for an English-speaking driver with a plush car or van. You can rent a motorcycle or scooter in most towns for less than $10. In the jungle areas, you can hire a motorized canoe and driver for under $50 a day, which works out cheaper for a group than signing up for a tour.

What Else?
• The four-day hike along the Inca Trail to Machu Picchu is a must for many travelers, but it now costs more than a lot of backpackers can spare. Plan months in advance to grab a spot. Costs for this trip have risen dramatically, yet demand still outstrips the limit of roughly 200 trekkers per day in high season. Expect to pay at least $500 a person for a trip with a reputable, responsible tour company in Cusco. This will include the Machu Picchu entrance fee, the train ticket back to Cusco, and all meals (which are surprisingly good and plentiful). Of course you could always book this trip with a company in your home country, for a mere two to ten times that price.
• Internet cafés are plentiful except in off the beaten path locations. A charge of $1 to $2 an hour is typical.
• White-water rafting trips are available near Arequipa and Huaraz, for around $25 to $40 per person.
• What to buy: alpaca sweaters, scarves gourd carvings, ponchos, finger puppets, hats, weavings, and Inca replicas that

range from authentic-looking to cheesy. You'll be accosted by vendors everywhere you go, so take your time and check the quality. If you don't want to haul souvenirs all over the country, you can find items from most regions in Lima before you leave. Prices for many items are cheaper in Ecuador and Bolivia, so wait if you're going to either of those.

• What you can buy for a buck or less: a beer at happy hour or in a store, two woven finger puppets, a wool hat or gloves, a half-hour of Internet access, many museum admissions, a big bowl of soup, a simple set lunch in a workers' restaurant or market, a glass of house wine, a huge bag of coca leaves.

THE AMERICAS

Ecuador

Ecuador is known as a good first stop for people coming to South America. This is partly because it has historically been a calm place to visit (in contrast to intermittent flare-ups in neighboring countries), and also because you can get to anywhere in a day from the capital, Quito. It's also downright cheap. All prices are in U.S. dollars, so there's never any worry about currency fluctuations if you're coming from the U.S. This keeps inflation low and prices stable.

It shares one similarity with many neighbors, however: Ecuador is blessed with an impressive variety of natural attractions. Massive mountains and volcanoes, a patch of jungle rainforest, Amazonian jungle, beaches, and colonial towns are all here. This small country boasts one of the highest concentrations of volcanoes in the world.

Quito used to be one of those capital cities that had an edge of danger and looked faded in the center rather than historic. All that has changed over the past decades as lots of restoration money has poured into Old Town. It's now a pleasant and relatively safe area filled with cafés and evocative hotels.

Atacames is the Ecuadorian beach vacation center, with the requisite thatched roof beach bars, drinks served in coconuts, and salsa parties at night. You can head out to the fringes of this scene and find quieter and cheaper abodes if you'd like. There are some beautiful secluded beaches tucked along other locations on the coast, especially in the Los Frailes nature reserve, but most take some work to get to. Montañita is a popular surf spot with the requisite cheap lodging and food. You can get a two-hour private surfing lesson for $15.

The Galapagos Islands are a fantastic experience you can't get anywhere else, but are a real budget buster, equivalent to months of travel on the mainland even if you go with the cheapest tour company. Save it for when you've got a few thousand dollars tucked away to spend on vacation.

The next best thing is to arrange a boat trip out to the protected Isla de la Plata, Machalilla National Park. Some agencies in the nearest town, Puerto Lopez, offer packages with snorkeling. This island offers a glimpse at some of the same creatures you'd find in the Galapagos, as well as some great whale watching during a few months of the year.

The market in Otavalo is on the "must see" list for visitors to Ecuador and is often thronged with tour groups. It's a real market for locals, however, so apart from having a good souvenir selection, it also offers a glimpse at how business is transacted here. If you stick around a while, you'll see that tradition still rules here and many people still wear traditional outfits. Besides, it's widely known that prices rise as soon as the tour buses pull in, and then fall as they depart. Spend the night here or in nearby Cotacachi to see a different side.

Cuenca is the country's cultural center and is becoming a foreigners' retirement center somewhere in between San Miguel de Allende in Mexico and Granada in Nicaragua in terms of foreign residents. Lots of travelers and expatriates are lured by the weather, the pace, and the beauty.

Baños has long been another popular gringo stop, with its hot springs, pleasant cafés, dramatic mountain views, and permanent spring climate.

Ecuador has imposed a series of protectionist measures that have raised prices on most imported goods, which includes most types of alcohol and electronics. Balance that out with subsidized fuel costs and this is still one of the best values on the planet in terms of what you can get for your money as a visitor.

A Coldwell Banker survey pegged Quito as the "most affordable international real estate market" in the world a few years back and *International Living* has frequently pegged Ecuador as the best retirement value anywhere. Prices have risen in Cuenca, but it's common—not an isolated case—to see houses with acres of land for sale in the country for less than $100K, condos (even in Quito) for under $50K, and apartments for rent for less than $250 a month. Spending at least $25,000 on real estate gets you a residency permit. Getting a maid is so cheap that no expats clean their own house and some residents report monthly bills under $800 a month—total. If you have to go to the hospital for a night, it'll cost you something like $270, not $10,000.

If you don't like the weather where you are in Ecuador, just change altitude. You climb higher to cool off, head to the beach or jungle to get warm.

Accommodation:

There are a few dozen hostels scattered around, with prices for a bed averaging $3 to $8. You can nearly always find a basic hotel room for less than $10, even in Quito, so the hostels are not such a find. In many towns, it's possible to find a double room with a shared bath for as little as $6.

Mid-range hotels are generally a good deal in Ecuador. Nice places with a private bath start at around $20 for a double and for $40 to $60 you can usually find a beautifully appointed hotel room in an interesting building. You can often get a large family suite for under $75. Except at the cheap places, you'll be hit with a service charge and tax, which combined can be as much as 25% of the room charge.

The beaches in Ecaudor are a bargain, with rooms on par with the prices in the rest of the country.

Top hotels here are a bargain by international standards. The best hotel is Cuenca is frequently $100 a night double and there are only two hotels in Quito that manage to consistently charge more than $200 a night.

The price of a jungle tour is in large part dependent on the quality and relative luxury of the lodge(s) you'll be staying in. They range from bamboo huts with a mattress to fancy eco-lodges for several hundred dollars a night per person (full board). Going for the very cheapest option, however, will often end up getting you exactly what you paid for, so do some research and choose well.

Food & Drink:

Ecuador has not really been known historically as a foodie destination, but as in Peru, many travelers are impressed with their meals here and chefs are reconstructing traditional Andean dishes to wow visitors. Some tour companies are even offering gastronomy tours of a week or more. Besides being able to grow nearly anything in this varied climate, the Ecuadorans also make great cheese, have plenty of seafood, and grow some of the world's best coffee and cocoa beans.

Soups are a specialty here. Locro soup, made with cheese, avocado, and potato, is a popular soup, as is one made with fish and vegetables and another with beef rib meat and potatoes or corn.

Aji (hot sauce) is a staple on most tables and many restaurants and families make their own. Pastries are cheap and plentiful.

Vegetarians will find plenty of choices throughout the country since the locals really eat their veggies here. Where tourists gather, you can find more creative endeavors that don't involve meat. Fish is plentiful on the coast, mostly served as ceviche. Avoiding red meat is no sweat here: it's not part of the daily diet outside the big cities.

Excellent fruit juices abound and are usually the best choice—reasonably priced, seasonal, and healthy. Finding good coffee is getting easier each year and on my last trip in late 2012, I rarely got a bad cup. If you drink it black, note that the traditional method is to boil coffee down to almost a syrup and then add lots of milk. So leave room for plenty of hot water otherwise. Beer is reasonably priced ($1 in a store, $1.50 to $2 in a basic bar/restaurant) and some local liquor brands are, but almost everything else is taxed at more than 100%. Prices are double what you see at home, even for Chilean wine, so a bottle of duty free whisky or wine is a great gift for a local.

A set meal in a local eatery can be as little as $1.50, including soup, main course, and dessert. You can find street snacks like corn pancakes and grilled corn for a few cents. If you don't mind eating unidentified animal organs, you can get all kinds of street food or market meals for a dollar or less. In restaurants geared to backpacking foreigners, you'll pay $2.50 to $6 for a meal, but this is usually several courses.

If you're self-catering, this is where the real bargains are. Excellent fruits and vegetables are in season all year, various breads are a bargain, and prices are a fraction of what you pay at home for eggs, meat, and cheese.

Transportation:

First, the price of gasoline: heavily subsidized from local production and gifts from Venezuela, it's around a dollar a gallon for diesel, two dollars for premium regular gas. So transportation is never going to be a big expense.

Buses are cheap, frequent, and ubiquitous. At times it may seem that everyone is on his or her way to somewhere. Local buses in Quito are a mere 25¢ and one out to the suburbs won't top 50¢.

For intercity ones, you can often stumble into a city bus terminal, say a single word (your destination), and be on your way a few minutes later. Some jingling dollar coins will likely cover your fare.

In theory, you can reach anywhere in the country in a day, but this assumes your bus doesn't break down and the mountainous roads don't wash out. For the sake of your long legs and comfort, take a "gringo bus" for long hauls. If a local bus is all that's available, it'll only be about a dollar an hour no matter where you're going. A doubling of that for a better bus is well worth it.

Until permanent (finally) repairs to train tracks are finished in mid-2013, taking a train is really a novelty trip for the ride's sake more than a means of transportation. Hopefully by the time you read this it'll be a different story as plans are to connect Quito and Guayaquil with several classes. This will be well worth the splurge since the scenery along these mountain tracks is fantastic and the "Devil's Nose" ride is something you won't find anywhere else.

Plane rides can shave off a lot of time. While you'll pay more than the locals do to get to the Galapagos ($450 or so round trip), prices are equal for all other routes. Flights are short too: Guayaquil from Quito takes less than an hour as is usually under $100 one-way. To Cuenca is shorter and around $75.

The roads are getting much better lately—half the reason the president is enjoying an unprecedented high approval rating. Renting a car is still not a great idea, so it's better to hire a car and driver for the day for $35 to $70.

A taxi ride in Quito or Guayaquil will seldom top $5 except from the airport. In smaller towns your tab is likely to be a couple dollars. Local bus rides are almost free and the more comfortable "executive" local bus will frequently be only about 10¢ to 15¢ more than the regular option.

What Else?

•   Ecuador is not short on heart pumping adventure options. Around the coastal town of Crucita, you can take tandem paragliding or hang gliding jaunts, or get certified to fly solo with a five-day course. You can also set up a combined rafting/jungle trek adventure in the East Andes or take a mountain biking trip where you only ride downhill!

•   In the "I'd be remiss if I didn't mention it" department, some people look up a local shaman, drink a brew made with some (legal) Ayahuasca vine, and are tripping out for a good 12 hours straight. Sometimes the native San Pedro cactus plant is used instead. If this is your scene, bring a friend you trust and head to Vilcabamba. Or ask around elsewhere. It's accepted as a cleansing ritual and is no secret.

• You'll get socked on the airport departure tax here, but it's usually included in your flight ticket now. Most nationalities don't have to pay a visa fee, which is a big advantage over Bolivia, Brazil, Chile, and Argentina.

• Jungle tours are roughly $40 to $75 per day each for most companies when it's booked locally, including food and lodging. At the top end, figure on ten times that to experience the 5,000 acres of Sacha Lodge.

• Apart from the Galapagos ($100 entrance), all national parks are now free.

• Staying well-groomed won't cost much: get a haircut and manicure for under $5 total.

• Bring an unlocked cell phone and get cheap calls. A SIM card is commonly $3 to $4 if you spend the equivalent amount in pre-paid minutes. Phone cabinas and Internet cafes are dirt-cheap otherwise. Wi-Fi is now common in hotels and many coffee shops.

• What to buy: thick woolen sweaters, ponchos, dolls in traditional outfits, leather goods, quality chocolate. Don't be fooled by the name: this is the home of the Panama Hat.

• What you can get for a buck or less: lunch at a market stall, four city bus rides, a short cab ride outside the cities, a bootleg CD or DVD, two ice cream cones or popsicles, 3 to 4 packages of crackers, a box of herbal teabags, a kilo of sugar, loaf of bread, 10 eggs, glass of fresh juice, two coffees, admission to some museums, two hours of Internet access, a bouquet of fresh flowers, a gallon of diesel fuel, enough bananas to feed your whole guesthouse.

THE AMERICAS

The Americas – Honorable Mentions

Mexico

Mexico is a big country. This is not some destination like Honduras or Bolivia where you can get from one side of the country to the other in one day. You could fit all of Central America in the southern half of Mexico and still have room to spare. In this vast space are wide varieties of geography, culture, attractions, and food.

Yet where do more than 75% of all foreign tourists go? To five resort areas: Puerto Vallarta, Los Cabos, Mazatlan, Acapulco, and the Cancun/Riviera Maya coast. These areas are not cheap. They can cost almost as much as a vacation at home, since everything is priced for foreign tourists on a quick vacation in the sun. For that reason, the country is in this honorable mentions section rather than having its own chapter.

The fact that Mexico has two rich neighbors to the north means that parts of the country are overdeveloped monstrosities and other areas represent a poor value (to put it nicely). In general, the beach resorts you see advertised in your local Sunday paper are set up for, and priced for, package tourists who are looking for little more than sun, sand, and nightlife. These spots can relieve some homesickness if you've been gone for a while, but otherwise they'll quickly deplete your budget and make you wonder how you woke up in Florida.

This is not to say that Mexico is not a good value. I have long had a modest little beach house in the Yucatan and when I go down there for a week or two, I feel like a rich man indeed. A nice beach, good meals for a few dollars and cheap beer— what else do you need? Then I moved to central Guanajuato with my family for a year and got even better deals day after day. Local transportation is not a screaming bargain, but it's quite comfortable and the roads are good. The people are wonderful, the towns are colorful, and the beaches are good. Plus you can often get a cheap flight from the U.S. or Canada for close to what you would pay for a domestic flight, despite nearly $100 in taxes and fees.

Read through some guidebooks, look at some photos online, and figure out how to see the real Mexico. Between Baja California on the west coast to the Yucatan Peninsula on the east coast, there are a hundred things to see and do. Sometimes it's just a matter of going a half-hour beyond the high-rise hotels, to Sayulita instead of Puerto Vallarta, Troncones instead of Ixtapa. Some of the highlights include the massive Copper Canyons, plenty of great lesser known beaches, picturesque colonial towns, amazing ruins, and mountains to explore. Your travels will also reveal a changing menu of food, music, and drinks.

You can spend a fortune in Mexico or you can scrape by for $30 per day. Between these two extremes, a backpacking couple looking for a reasonable level of comfort would generally do okay on $50 to $80 a day and mid-range travelers can live quite well in most areas on $90 to $200 per day for a couple, especially in the interior. The biggest budget buster here is transportation, so lots of long overnight buses will quickly increase the average.

Argentina

The country of Argentina was coming off a wrenching crisis when I put out the first edition of this book, after defaulting on $100 billion in foreign debt and losing its 1-to-1-peso peg to the dollar. So it was one of the greatest deals on the planet. Over the years, persistent double-digit inflation, bad monetary decisions, and lots of anti-tourist moves have made the country less attractive, so I've moved it into the Honorable Mentions section. It's still a good value if you're a mid-range traveler or couple, but has gotten much more expensive for backpackers and families.

In between editions, the government raided national pensions to prop up spending, put some of the tightest controls in the world on imports (causing many foreign brands to give up and leave), and made foreign exchange difficult to keep people from cashing in pesos for dollars every payday. This makes things tough for foreign visitors, who can't even get a day's expenses out of the ATM. Adding insult to injury, they instituted a reciprocal visa fee, meaning Americans and Canadians pay well over $130 just to enter the country by air. For an American Family of four, the cost to visit Argentina is more than $500 before even stepping out of the airport.

Because of high entry charges, rising hotel prices, expensive domestic flights, and high inflation, my estimated daily budget has nearly doubled in four years. Backpackers should budget $40 to $75 per day single or $60 to $120 double if here for a few weeks or more. As always, it depends on how much you are moving around and what part of the country you are in. If all your time is in the capital and resort areas over a week or less, it'll be at the high end—or more. If you spend a couple weeks in the northwest around Salta and Cafayate, your costs will be significantly lower.

If you are on a mid-range or upper-range budget, you will eat incredible meals on what would be a fast-food budget at home, and drink bottles of wine at restaurants for less than a glass of Malbec costs at the closest wine bar to your house. If you can afford to bump up your budget for a few weeks somewhere, this is a place where you'll get a great return at mealtime. On a budget of $120 to $200 a couple, you can have a comfortably good time.

Here's the thing: as this book went to press, many experts were predicting another meltdown in Argentina, based on a long list of warning signs. (For one thing, there's a shadow money exchange system again, paying 50% more than the official rate—bring cash.) If it all goes south again as it did in the early 00s, it'll be opportunity time again for foreigners. Another reason to keep an eye on the international news!

Panama

The country perpetually known as "like Costa Rica 20 years ago" is not as cheap as Honduras and Nicaragua, but it is a much better deal than Costa Rica. Since it shares many of the same attributes and actually has more of an indigenous culture, it's worth a visit.

An amazing 29% of the land in Panama is protected as national parks, forest reserves, and wildlife sanctuaries. More than 900 species of birds call Panama home, as do 220 species of mammals and 354 species of reptiles and amphibians. Plus, the offshore area hosts hundreds of islands and miles of protected coral reef, sheltering a wide diversity of marine life.
Panama won't stay undiscovered forever, but this is one of the best places to beat the crowds—without having to rough it as a trailblazing pioneer. At some point, the spotlights of glossy travel magazines and influential websites will light the way, and the throngs will follow.

This is an easy place in which to travel. Because of the long U.S. presence, English is fairly common. The U.S. dollar has been the Panamanian currency since 1903. Roads are well maintained and in the cities you can drink the water.

The main reason the country is not a great bargain is the lack of cheap accommodation. Since there haven't been all that many visitors, there's a shortage of non-business hotels, especially in the capital. This keeps prices higher than they should be. Apart from that, however, Panama won't hit your wallet too hard. I've had beers at a waterfront bar for 30¢ each, and eaten great sit-down lunches that were $2.50. You can call home for 5¢ a minute or log onto the Internet for an hour for 75¢. A pound of bananas is 20¢. Because the country has few import restrictions or taxes, it has some of the cheapest booze and wine in the world. If you're looking for a place to party for cheap, head to Panama.

Getting around is not expensive either. The cheapest buses between cities run a little more than a dollar an hour, but doubling this will get you onto a nice executive bus that's comfortable. There's also an efficient working train between the two main cities on opposite coasts.

Just remember that the capital is a major business center that is nicknamed the "crossroads of the Americas" for a good reason. Prices are significantly higher there than in the rest of the country and you'll spend a lot on taxis. So fly in, spend a couple nights there, and then head out.

RESOURCES

You want resources? Go to the website at www.WorldsCheapestDestinations.com and click away.

Looking up the things that used to fill whole chapters of books like this is now much easier to do on the web. The sheer volume of it all can be overwhelming, and a Google search will put well-funded corporate sites (and Google-owned sites) at the top of the rankings, often leaving better sources of content fighting to get your attention.

Because the first edition of this book came out at the end of 2002, the accompanying website has years of refinement built into it for listings. Since it is continually updated, it is a better resource than anything I could put into this book.

For recommendations that are geared to adventurous budget travelers, go to the website listed here and just click on the resources links for the following:

- Budget Travel Web Sites
- Travel Magazines
- Recommended Travel Books
- Overseas Living (Working, Studying, Volunteering)
- Travel Hosts, Home Exchange, and Villa Rentals
- Cheap Flights and Travel Moneysavers
- Special Needs, Requirements, and Desires
- Travel Gear Stores and Sites
- Bargain Destination Articles
- Travel News Links

Also, see twice-weekly updates on the Cheapest Destinations blog at CheapestDestinationsBlog.com

However, if you're looking for a shortcut, here are a few "heavy hitter" resources that I turn to over and over for advice and price information. For individual countries, however, your best bet is a good guidebook and a content-rich website focused on a single destination. (And usually the guidebook will point you to those useful websites.)

Bookmark these and come back to them because they're far more useful than what comes up in the top of Google search results these days.

Resource Websites
LonelyPlanet.com
SmarterTravel.com
BudgetTravel.com
ConsumerTraveler.com
Bootsnall.com
MatadorNetwork.com
Moon.com
Travelfish.org (for Southeast Asia)
SAExplorers.org (for South America)
Seat61.com (for train travel)
JohnnyJet.com
TransitionsAbroad.com

Also, see ContrarianTraveler.com and follow the resources link for a list of great budget travel blogs. There are way too many to list here.

Books
Check out the most recent edition of the following for sage advice on traveling around the world and working abroad. You can find links to them at the worldscheapestdestinations.com site.

Vagabonding, by Rolf Potts
Rough Guides First Time Around the World, by Doug Lansky
Rough Guides First Time in Europe
Rough Guides First Time in Asia
Traveler's Tool Kit: Mexico and Central America, by Tim Leffel and Rob Sangster

Make Your Travel Dollars Worth a Fortune, by Tim Leffel
The Practical Nomad, by Edward Hasbrouck
Work Your Way Around the World, by Susan Griffith (she is also the author of *Gap Years for Grown-ups* and *Your Gap Year.*)
The Big Guide to Living and Working Overseas, by Jean-Marc Hachey
How to Travel for Free (or pretty damn near it!), by Shelley Seale and Keith Hajovsky
Travel Happy, Budget Low, by Susanna Zaraysky

ABOUT THE AUTHOR

Tim Leffel is a full-time writer and editor who has dispatched travel articles from dozens of countries on five continents. He is the founder and editor of several popular websites including Practical Travel Gear and his Cheapest Destinations Blog. He has written for a wide range of print and online publications such as *Arthur Frommer's Budget Travel*, LonelyPlanet.com, the *Boston Globe, Global Traveler*, and *Imbibe*. He is also the editor of the travel narrative site PerceptiveTravel.com, an award-winning publication that is home to some of the best wandering authors in the world.

Besides the three previous editions of this book, he has also published *Make Your Travel Dollars Worth a Fortune: A Contrarian Travel Guide to Getting More for Less*, on Travelers' Tales Publishing and *Traveler's Tool Kit: Mexico and Central America*, co-written by Rob Sangster, on Menasha Ridge. His *Travel Writing 2.0* book is one of the most popular titles on finding success as a wandering writer or blogger.

He has also contributed as a collaborator or ghostwriter to seven business books. He has at times been called a proposal writer, hotel reviewer, ESL teacher, sales manager, music biz marketer, ski instructor, and plenty more titles that will someday make a nice business card collage on the wall.

When not traveling on assignment, Leffel lives in either Tampa, Florida or Guanajuato, Mexico. To see more about what the author is working on, go to www.TimLeffel.com.

The author appears frequently in the major media as a travel expert and is available for interviews. He is also happy to answer any questions this book has raised for readers. Click on the "contact" button at his websites, including the following: www.timleffel.com.

ACKNOWLEDGEMENTS

First and foremost, I want to thank all the people who bought the first three editions of this book. Thankfully there were enough of you—even without my friends and relatives getting a copy—that it is possible to keep the series going with regular updates.

I've been to every country in this book, but there's no way to visit all of them on a regular basis. Thanks to all the travelers and bloggers out there who have opened up their budget to show what they've been spending so I could get a reality check.

I have to thank Mom for passing on a few of her creative genes, and Dad for resisting the temptation to tell me what to do with my life. Thanks to Donna for making me get out of an office chair to go globetrotting in the first place, and now putting up with my travel absences as a result of me making a living from it. Thanks to Alina for reminding me that anything can be an adventure when seen through a child's eyes, even when only a few blocks from home.

On the professional side, thanks to Angela and Richard at Booklocker for continuing to make this book a commercial success outside the old inefficient "way it's done" traditional publishing system. Vickilyn Crawford did the proofing, MarketShare Masters handled cover design.

Thanks to all the editors who keep giving me writing work, the journalists who track me down for cheap travel advice, the advertisers who keep the wheels humming, and the blog and website readers who keep tuning in. I'm gracious to my fellow travel authors for contributing to the Perceptive Travel site and for being a great help in other ways. You know who you are.

CPSIA information can be obtained at www.ICGtesting.com
Printed in the USA
LVOW07s1519011013

354946LV00016B/940/P